# FINANCIAL PLANNERS, INVESTMENT ADVISERS AND BROKER-DEALERS

## OVERSIGHT AND ACCESS TO REGISTRATION INFORMATION

# FINANCIAL INSTITUTIONS AND SERVICES

Additional books in this series can be found on Nova's website under the Series tab.

Additional E-books in this series can be found on Nova's website under the E-book tab.

FINANCIAL INSTITUTIONS AND SERVICES

# FINANCIAL PLANNERS, INVESTMENT ADVISERS AND BROKER-DEALERS

## OVERSIGHT AND ACCESS TO REGISTRATION INFORMATION


TAYLOR DAVIS
AND
GRAHAM S. CRAWFORD
EDITORS



NOVINKA

*New York*

For permission to use material from this book please contact us:
Telephone 631-231-7269; Fax 631-231-8175
Web Site: http://www.novapublishers.com



**LIBRARY OF CONGRESS CATALOGING-IN-PUBLICATION DATA**

ISBN: 978-1-62257-837-5

*Published by Nova Science Publishers, Inc. † New York*

# CONTENTS

# PREFACE

Consumers are increasingly turning for help to financial planners--individuals who help clients meet their financial goals by providing assistance with such things as selecting investments and insurance products, and managing tax and estate planning. This book examines how financial planners, investment advisers and broker-dealers are regulated and overseen at the federal and state levels; what is known about the effectiveness of this regulation; and the advantages and disadvantages of alternative regulatory approaches.

Chapter 1 – Consumers are increasingly turning for help to financial planners— individuals who help clients meet their financial goals by providing assistance with such things as selecting investments and insurance products, and managing tax and estate planning. The Dodd-Frank Wall Street Reform and Consumer Protection Act mandated that GAO study the oversight of financial planners. This report examines (1) how financial planners are regulated and overseen at the federal and state levels, (2) what is known about the effectiveness of this regulation, and (3) the advantages and disadvantages of alternative regulatory approaches. To address these objectives, GAO reviewed federal and state statutes and regulations, analyzed complaint and enforcement activity, and interviewed federal and state government entities and organizations representing financial planners, various other arms of the financial services industry, and consumers.

Chapter 2 – The Dodd-Frank Wall Street Reform and Consumer Protection Act (the "Dodd-Frank Act" or "Act") was signed into law on July 21, 2010. Section 919B of the Act directs the Securities and Exchange Commission (the "Commission" or "SEC") to complete a study, including recommendations, of ways to improve the access of investors to registration information about registered and previously registered investment advisers, associated persons of investment advisers, brokers and dealers and their associated persons, and to identify additional information that should be made publicly available. The Act specifies that the study include an analysis of the advantages and disadvantages of further centralizing access to registration information, and identify data pertinent to investors and the method and format for displaying and publishing the data to enhance the information's accessibility and utility to investors. The Act requires the Commission to complete the study within six months after the date of enactment of the Act (*i.e.*, by January 21, 2011), and to implement any recommendations within eighteen months after completion of the study.

In: Financial Planners, Investment Advisers ... ISBN: 978-1-62257-837-5
Editors: T. Davis and G. S. Crawford 

*Chapter 1*

# CONSUMER FINANCE: REGULATORY COVERAGE GENERALLY EXISTS FOR FINANCIAL PLANNERS, BUT CONSUMER PROTECTION ISSUES REMAIN*

***United States Government Accountability Office***

## WHY GAO DID THIS STUDY

Consumers are increasingly turning for help to financial planners—individuals who help clients meet their financial goals by providing assistance with such things as selecting investments and insurance products, and managing tax and estate planning. The Dodd-Frank Wall Street Reform and Consumer Protection Act mandated that GAO study the oversight of financial planners. This report examines (1) how financial planners are regulated and overseen at the federal and state levels, (2) what is known about the effectiveness of this regulation, and (3) the advantages and disadvantages of alternative regulatory approaches. To address these objectives, GAO reviewed federal and state statutes and regulations, analyzed complaint and enforcement

* This is an edited, reformatted and augmented version of the Highlights of GAO-11-235, a report to congressional addressees, dated January 2011.

activity, and interviewed federal and state government entities and organizations representing financial planners, various other arms of the financial services industry, and consumers.

## WHAT GAO RECOMMENDS

GAO recommends that (1) NAIC assess consumers' understanding of the standards of care associated with the sale of insurance products, (2) SEC assess investors' understanding of financial planners' titles and designations, and (3) SEC collaborate with the states to identify methods to better understand problems associated specifically with the financial planning activities of investment advisers. NAIC said it would consider GAO's recommendation and SEC provided no comments.

## WHAT GAO FOUND

There is no specific, direct regulation of "financial planners" *per se* at the federal or state level, but various laws and regulations apply to most of the services they provide. Financial planners are primarily regulated as investment advisers by the Securities and Exchange Commission (SEC) and the states, and are subject to laws and regulation governing broker-dealers and insurance agents when they act in those capacities. Federal and state agencies have regulations on marketing and the use of titles and designations that also can apply to financial planners.

The regulatory structure applicable to financial planners covers the great majority of their services, but the attention paid to enforcing existing regulation can vary and certain consumer protection issues remain. First, consumers may be unclear about when a financial planner is required to serve the client's best interest, particularly when the same financial planner provides multiple services associated with different standards of care. SEC is studying these issues with regard to securities transactions, but no complementary review is under way by the National Association of Insurance Commissioners (NAIC) related to the sale of high-risk insurance products. Second, financial planners can adopt numerous titles and designations, which vary greatly in the expertise or training that they signify, but consumers may not understand or be able to distinguish among them. SEC has a mandated review under way on financial literacy among investors and incorporating this issue into that review could assist in assessing further changes that may be needed. Finally, the extent of problems related to financial planners is not fully known because SEC generally does not track data on complaints, examination results, and enforcement activities associated with financial planners specifically, and distinct from investment advisers as a whole. A regulatory system should have data to identify risks and problem areas, and given that financial planning is a growing industry that has raised certain consumer protection issues, regulators could benefit from better information on the extent of problems specifically involving financial planning services.

A number of stakeholders have proposed different approaches to the regulation of financial planners, including (1) creation of a federally chartered board overseeing financial planners as a distinct profession; (2) augmenting oversight of investment advisers with a self-regulatory organization; (3) extending the fiduciary standard of care to more financial services professionals; and (4) specifying standards for financial planners and the designations that they use. While the views of stakeholder interests vary, a majority of the regulatory agencies and financial services industry representatives GAO spoke with did not favor significant structural change to the overall regulation of financial planners because they said existing regulation provides adequate coverage of most financial planning activities. Given available information, an additional layer of regulation specific to financial planners does not appear to be warranted at this time.

## ABBREVIATIONS

| | |
|---|---|
| Advisers Act | Investment Advisers Act of 1940 |
| Dodd-Frank Act | Dodd-Frank Wall Street Reform and Consumer Protection Act |
| FINRA | Financial Industry Regulatory Authority |
| Form ADV | Uniform Application for Investment Adviser Registration |
| FTC | Federal Trade Commission |
| NAIC | National Association of Insurance Commissioners |
| NASAA | North American Securities Administrators Association |
| SEC | Securities and Exchange Commission |

January 18, 2011

Congressional Addressees

Consumers are increasingly turning for help to professionals who describe themselves as financial planners for assistance with a broad range of services, such as selecting the right balance of stocks and bonds for an investment portfolio, choosing among insurance products, and tax and estate planning. Although there is no statutory or single definition of financial planning, it can be broadly defined as a systematic process that individuals use to achieve their financial goals. Between 2000 and 2008, the number of financial planners more than doubled and may continue to climb as more individuals are asked to take responsibility for their retirement savings and must choose among a growing array of investment options.

Some financial planning organizations have raised concerns that no single law governs providers of financial planning services, broadly describing this situation as a regulatory gap. Concerns also exist that financial planners may have an inherent conflict of interest in recommending products they may stand to benefit from selling. In addition, some consumer advocates believe consumers may be confused by the numerous titles and designations that financial planners can use. This report responds to a mandate included in Section 919C of the Dodd-Frank Wall Street Reform and Consumer Protection Act (Dodd-Frank Act) that directed GAO to conduct a study on the oversight and regulation of financial planners. Our objectives are to address (1) how financial planners are regulated and overseen at the federal and state levels, (2) what is known about the effectiveness of regulation of financial planners and what regulatory gaps or overlap may exist, and (3) alternative approaches for the regulation of financial planners and the advantages and disadvantages of these approaches.

To address these objectives, we reviewed federal and selected state statutes and regulations applicable to financial planners. We also reviewed regulations issued by the Securities and Exchange Commission (SEC) and the Financial Industry Regulatory Authority (FINRA), and model laws developed by the National Association of Insurance Commissioners (NAIC) and by the North American Securities Administrators Association (NASAA). In addition, we reviewed applicable securities and insurance laws and regulations of five states—California, Illinois, North Carolina, Pennsylvania, and Texas. We also interviewed representatives of, and gathered documentation from, SEC, FINRA, the Federal Trade Commission (FTC), NAIC, and organizations representing the interests of consumers, financial planners, and various arms of the financial services industry. In addition, we gathered information on complaints and enforcement activity, as available, from SEC, FINRA, FTC, and selected state regulators and organizations. A more extensive discussion of our scope and methodology appears in appendix I.

We conducted this performance audit from June 2010 to January 2011 in accordance with generally accepted government auditing standards. Those standards require that we plan and perform the audit to obtain sufficient, appropriate evidence to provide a reasonable basis for our findings and conclusions based on our audit objectives. We believe that the evidence obtained provides a reasonable basis for our findings and conclusions based on our audit objectives.

## BACKGROUND

Financial planning typically involves a variety of services, including preparing financial plans for clients based on their financial circumstances and objectives and making recommendations for specific actions clients may take. In many cases, financial planners also help implement these recommendations by, for example, providing insurance products, securities, or other investments. Individuals who provide financial planning services may call themselves a variety of different titles, such as financial planner, financial consultant, financial adviser, trust advisor, or wealth manager. In addition, many financial planners have privately conferred professional designations or certifications, such as Certified Financial Planner®, Chartered Financial Consultant®, or Personal Financial Specialist.

The number of financial planners in the United States rose from approximately 94,000 in 2000 to 208,400 in 2008, according to the Bureau of Labor Statistics. The bureau projects the number will rise to 271,200 by 2018 because of the need for advisers to assist the millions of workers expected to retire in the next 10 years.[1] According to the bureau, 29 percent of financial planners are self-employed and the remaining 71 percent are employees of firms, some of them large entities with offices nationwide that provide a variety of financial services. The median annual wage for financial planners was $68,200 in May 2009.

According to an analysis of the 2007 Survey of Consumer Finances, the most recent year for which survey results are available, in 2007 about 22 percent of U.S. households used a financial planner for investment and saving decisions and about 12 percent of U.S. households used a financial planner for making credit and borrowing decisions. Those households most likely to use a financial planner were those with higher incomes. For example, 37 percent of households in the top income quartile used a financial planner to make investment and saving decisions compared to 10 percent of households in the bottom quartile.[2]

## VARIOUS FEDERAL AND STATE LAWS AND REGULATIONS APPLY TO FINANCIAL PLANNERS AND THEIR ACTIVITIES

Financial planners are primarily regulated by federal and state investment adviser laws, because planners typically provide advice about securities as part of their business. In addition, financial planners that sell securities or insurance products are subject to applicable laws governing broker-dealers and insurance agents. Certain laws and regulations can also apply to the use of the titles, designations, and marketing materials that financial planners use.

### Financial Planners Are Primarily Regulated by Federal and State Investment Adviser Laws

There is no specific, direct regulation of "financial planners" *per se* at the federal or state level. However, the activities of financial planners are primarily regulated under federal and state laws and regulations governing investment advisers—that is, individuals or firms that provide investment advice about securities for compensation. According to SEC staff, financial planning normally includes making general or specific recommendations about securities, insurance, savings, and anticipated retirement.[3] SEC has issued guidance that broadly interprets the Investment Advisers Act of 1940 (Advisers Act) to apply to most financial planners, because the advisory services they offer clients typically include providing advice about securities for compensation.[4] Similarly, NASAA representatives told us that states take a similar approach on the application of investment adviser laws to financial planners and, as a result, generally register and oversee financial planners as investment advisers. As investment advisers, financial planners are subject to a fiduciary standard of care when they provide advisory services, so that the planner "[is] held to the highest standards of conduct and must act in the best interest of [the adviser's] clients."[5]

SEC and state securities departments share responsibility for the oversight of investment advisers in accordance with the Advisers Act.[6] Under that act, SEC generally oversees investment adviser firms that manage $25 million or more in client assets, and the states that require registration oversee those firms that manage less.[7] However, as a result of section 410 of the Dodd-Frank Act, as of July 2011 the states generally will have registration and oversight responsibilities for investment adviser firms that manage less than $100 million in client assets, instead of firms that manage less than $25 million in assets as under current law.[8] This will result in the states gaining responsibility for firms with assets under management between $25 million and $100 million. As shown in figure 1, as of October 2010, of the approximately 16,000 investment adviser firms providing financial planning services, the states were overseeing about 11,100 firms and SEC was overseeing about 4,900 such firms.[9] However, in July 2011 about 2,400 of investment adviser firms that provided financial planning services (15 percent of the 16,000 firms) may shift from SEC to state oversight.[10]

SEC's supervision of investment adviser firms includes evaluating their compliance with federal securities laws by conducting examinations of firms—including reviewing disclosures made to customers—and investigating and imposing sanctions for violations of securities laws. According to SEC staff, in its examinations, the agency takes specific steps to review the financial planning services of investment advisers. For example, SEC may review a sample of financial plans that the firm prepared for its customers to check whether the firm's advice and investment recommendations are consistent with customers' goals, the contract with the firm, and the firm's disclosures.

However, the frequency with which SEC conducts these examinations varies, largely because of resource constraints faced by the agency.[11] SEC staff told us that the agency examined only about 10 percent of the investment advisers it supervises in 2009. In addition, they noted that generally an investment adviser is examined, on average, every 12 to 15 years, although firms considered to be of higher risk are examined more frequently. In 2007, we noted that harmful practices could go undetected because investment adviser firms rated lower-risk are unlikely to undergo routine examinations within a reasonable period of time, if at all.[12]

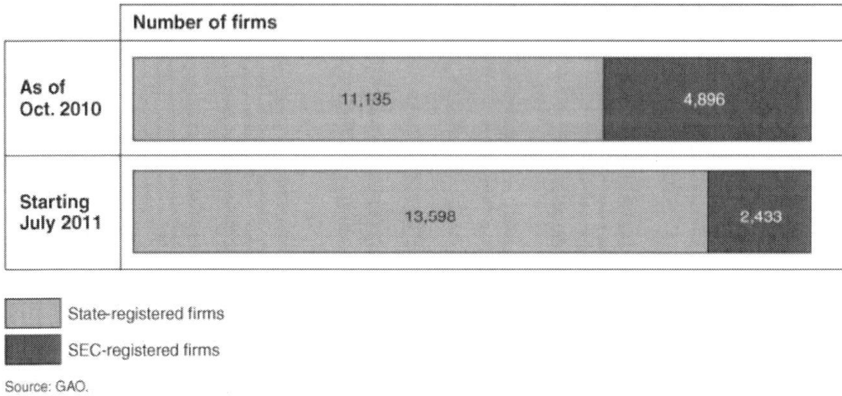


Figure 1. Change in Regulatory Oversight of Investment Adviser Firms Providing Financial Planning Services as a Result of the Dodd-Frank Act.

According to NASAA, state oversight of investment adviser firms generally includes activities similar to those undertaken by SEC, including taking specific steps to review a firm's financial planning services. According to NASAA, states generally register not just investment adviser firms but also investment adviser representatives—that is, individuals who provide investment advice and work for a state- or federally registered investment adviser firm.[13]

## Financial Planners Are Subject to Broker-Dealer and Insurance Laws When Acting in Those Capacities

In addition to providing advisory services, such as developing a financial plan, financial planners generally help clients implement the plan by making specific recommendations and by selling securities, insurance products, and other investments. SEC data show that, as of October 2010, 19 percent of investment adviser firms that provided financial planning services also provided brokerage services, and 27 percent provided insurance.[14]

Financial planners that provide brokerage services, such as buying or selling stocks, bonds, or mutual fund shares, are subject to broker-dealer regulation at the federal and state levels. At the federal level, SEC oversees U.S. broker-dealers, and SEC's oversight is supplemented by self-regulatory organizations (SRO).[15] The primary SRO for broker-dealers is FINRA. State securities offices work in conjunction with SEC and FINRA to regulate securities firms. Salespersons working for broker-dealers are subject to state registration requirements, including examinations. About half of broker-dealers were examined in 2009 by SEC and SROs. Under broker-dealer regulation, financial planners are held to a suitability standard of care when making a recommendation to a client to buy or sell a security, meaning that they must recommend those securities that they reasonably believe are suitable for the customer.[16]

Financial planners that sell insurance products, such as life insurance or annuities, must be licensed by the states to sell these products and are subject to state insurance regulation. In contrast to securities entities (other than national banks) that are subject to dual federal and state oversight, the states are generally responsible for regulating the business of insurance. When acting as insurance agents, financial planners are subject to state standard of care requirements, which can vary by product and by state. As of October 2010, 32 states had adopted a previous version of the NAIC Suitability in Annuities Transactions Model Regulation, according to NAIC.[17] In general, this regulation requires insurance agents to appropriately address consumers' insurance needs and financial objectives at the time of an annuity transaction.[18] Thirty-four states had also adopted the Life Insurance Disclosure Model Regulation in a uniform and substantially similar manner as of July 2010, according to NAIC. This regulation does not include a suitability requirement, although it does require insurers to provide customers with information that will improve their ability to select the most appropriate life insurance plan for their needs and improve their understanding of the policy's basic features.

Financial planners that sell variable insurance products, such as variable life insurance or variable annuities, are subject to both state insurance regulation and broker-dealer regulation, because these products are regulated as both securities and insurance products. When selling variable insurance, financial planners are subject to FINRA sales practice standards requiring that such sales be subject to suitability standards.[19] In addition, other FINRA rules and guidance, such as those governing standards for communication with the public, apply to the sale of variable insurance products.[20] In addition, as previously discussed, 32 states also generally require insurance agents and companies to appropriately address a consumer's insurance needs and financial objectives at the time of an annuity transaction. However, in the past, we have reported that the effectiveness of market conduct regulation—that is, examination of the sales practices and behavior of insurers—may be limited by a lack of reciprocity and uniformity, which may lead to uneven consumer protection across states.[21]

## Federal and State Laws and Regulations Can Apply to the Use of Marketing Materials and Financial Planning Titles and Designations

At the federal level, SEC and FINRA have regulations on advertising and standards of communication that apply to the strategies investment adviser firms and broker-dealers use to market their financial planning services. For example, SEC-registered investment advisers must follow SEC regulations on advertising and other communications, which prohibit false or misleading advertisements, and these regulations apply to investment advisers' marketing of financial planning services.[22] FINRA regulations on standards for communication with the public similarly prohibit false, exaggerated, unwarranted, or misleading statements or claims by broker-dealers, and broker-dealer advertisements are subject to additional approval, filing, and recordkeeping requirements and review procedures.[23] According to many company officials we spoke with, their companies responded to these requirements by putting procedures in place to determine which designations and titles their registered representatives may use in their marketing materials, such as business cards.

SEC and state securities regulators also regulate information that investment advisers are required to disclose to their clients. In the Uniform Application for Investment Adviser Registration (Form ADV), regulators have typically required investment adviser firms to provide new and prospective clients with background information, such as the basis of the advisory fees, types of services provided (such as financial planning services), and strategies for addressing conflicts of interest that may arise from their business activities.[24] Recent changes to Form ADV are designed to improve the disclosures that firms provide to clients. For example, firms must now provide clients with information about the advisory personnel on whom they rely for investment advice, including the requirements and applicability of any professional designations or certifications advisers may choose to include in their background information.

Most states regulate the use of the title "financial planner," and state securities and insurance laws can apply to the misuse of this title and other titles. For example, according to NASAA, at least 29 states specifically include financial planners in their definition of investment adviser.[25] According to NAIC, in many states, regulators can use unfair trade practice laws to prohibit insurance agents from holding themselves out as financial planners when in fact they are only engaged in the sale of life or annuity insurance products. However, as noted earlier, the effectiveness of the regulation of insurers' market conduct varies across states. In particular, in 2010 we noted inconsistencies in the state regulation of life settlements, a potentially high-risk transaction in which financial planners may participate.[26]

In addition, we were told some states had adopted regulations limiting the use of "senior-specific designations"—that is, designations that imply expertise or special training in advising senior citizen or elderly investors. According to NAIC, as of December 2010, 25 states had adopted in a uniform and substantially similar manner the NAIC Model Regulation on the Use of Senior-Specific Certifications and Professional Designations in the Sale of Life Insurance and Annuities, which limits the use of senior-specific designations by insurance agents. According to NASAA, as of December 2010, 31 states had adopted—and at least 9 other states were planning to adopt—the NASAA Model Rule on the Use of Senior-Specific Certifications and Professional Designations, which prohibits the misleading use of senior-specific designations by investment adviser representatives and other financial professionals.

# REGULATORY STRUCTURE FOR FINANCIAL PLANNERS COVERS MOST ACTIVITIES, BUT SOME CONSUMER PROTECTION ISSUES EXIST, AND DATA TRACKING COMPLAINTS AND REGULATORY ACTIONS AGAINST PLANNERS ARE LIMITED

The regulatory system for financial planners covers most activities in which they engage. However, enforcement of regulation may be inconsistent and some questions exist about consumers' understanding of the roles, standards of care, and titles and designations that a financial planner may have. The ability of regulators to identify potential problems is limited because they do not specifically track complaints, inspections, and enforcement actions specific to financial planning services.

## Existing Regulation Covers Most Financial Planning Services

Although there is no single stand-alone regulatory body with oversight of financial planners, the regulatory structure for financial planners covers most activities in which they engage. As discussed earlier, and summarized in figure 2, the primary activities a financial planner performs are subject to existing regulation at the federal or state level, primarily through regulation pertaining to investment advisers, broker-dealers, and insurance agents. As such, SEC, FINRA, and NASAA staff, a majority of state securities regulators, financial industry representatives, consumer groups, and academic and subject matter experts with whom we spoke said that, in general, they believe the regulatory structure for financial planners is comprehensive, although, as discussed below, the attention paid to enforcing existing regulation has varied.

As noted earlier, the activities a financial planner normally engages in generally include advice related to securities—and such activities make financial planners subject to regulation under the Advisers Act. One industry association and an academic expert noted that it would be very difficult to provide financial planning services without offering investment advice or considering securities. SEC staff told us that financial planners holding even broad discussions of securities—for example, what proportion of a portfolio should be invested in stocks—would be required to register as investment advisers or investment adviser representatives. In theory, a financial planner could offer only services that do not fall under existing regulatory regimes—for example, advice on household budgeting—but such an example is likely hypothetical and such a business model may be hard to sustain. SEC and NASAA staff, a majority of the state securities regulators we spoke with, and many representatives of the financial services industry told us that they were not aware of any individuals serving as financial planners who were not regulated as investment advisers or regulated under another regulatory regime. Some regulators and industry representatives also said that, to the extent that financial planners offered services that did not fall under such regulation, the new Bureau of Consumer Financial Protection potentially could have jurisdiction over such services.[27]

However, not everyone agreed that regulation of financial planners was comprehensive. One group, the Financial Planning Coalition, has argued that a regulatory gap exists because no single law governs the delivery of the broad array of financial advice to the public.[28] According to the coalition, the provision of integrated financial advice—which would cover topics such as selecting and managing investments, income taxes, saving for college, home ownership, retirement, insurance, and estate planning—is unregulated. Instead, the coalition says that there is patchwork regulation of financial planning advice, and it views having two sets of laws—one regulating the provision of investment advice and another regulating the sale of products—as problematic.

In addition, although the regulatory structure itself for financial planners may generally be comprehensive, attention paid to enforcing existing statute and regulation has varied. For example, as noted earlier, due to resource constraints, the examination of SEC-supervised investment advisers is infrequent. Further, as also noted earlier, market conduct regulation of insurers—which would include the examination of the sales practices and behavior of financial planners selling insurance products—has been inconsistent. Some representatives of industry associations told us that they believed that a better alternative to additional regulation of financial planners would be increased enforcement of existing law and regulation, particularly related to fraud and unfair trade practices.

Certain professionals—including attorneys, certified public accountants, broker-dealers, and teachers—who provide financial planning advice are exempt from regulation under the Advisers Act if such advice is "solely incidental" to their other business activities.[29] According to an SEC staff interpretation, this exemption would not apply to individuals who held themselves out to the public as providing financial planning services, and would apply only to individuals who provided specific investment advice on anything other than "rare, isolated and non-periodic instances."[30] Banks and bank employees are also excluded from the Advisers Act and are subject to separate banking regulation.[31] The American Bankers Association told us that the financial planning activities of bank employees such as trust advisors or wealth managers were typically utilized by clients with more than $5 million in investable assets. The association noted that these activities were subject to a fiduciary standard and the applicable supervision of federal and state banking regulators.

Most regulators and academic experts and many financial services industry representatives we spoke with told us that there is some overlap in the regulation of individuals who serve as financial planners because such individuals might be subject to oversight by different regulatory bodies for the different services they provide. For example, a financial planner who recommends and sells variable annuities as part of a financial plan is regulated as a registered representative of a broker-dealer as well as an insurance agent under applicable federal and state laws. However, some state regulators we spoke with told us that such overlap may be appropriate since the regulatory regimes cover different functional areas.

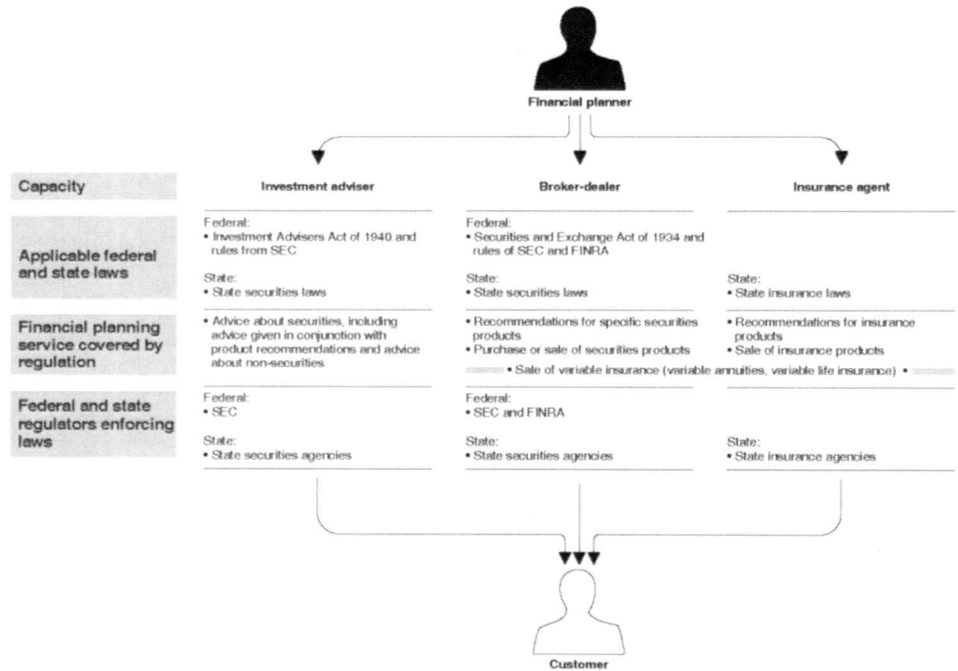


Source: GAO.

Note: This figure highlights three major areas of regulatory oversight but is not comprehensive and does not include other regulatory regimes or practice standards that may be applicable to financial planners. In addition, not all investment advisers, broker-dealers, or insurance agents are financial planners.

Figure 2. Summary of Key Statutes and Regulations That Can Apply to Financial Planners.

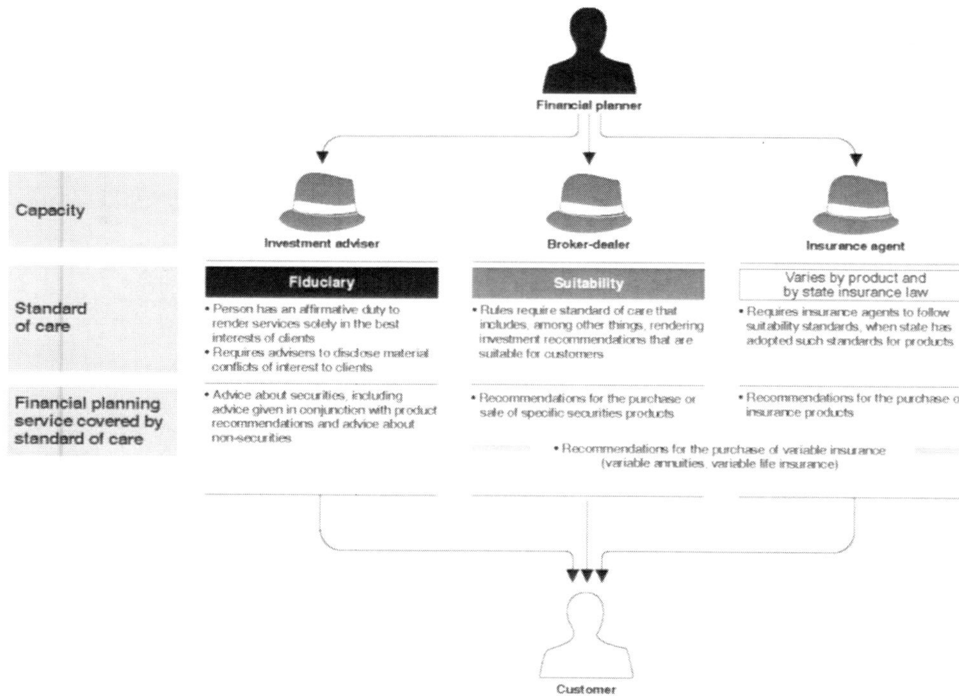


Source: GAO.

Note: This figure is illustrative and is not comprehensive: financial planners may serve in capacities other than those shown here, and not all investment advisers, broker-dealers, and insurance agents serve as financial planners.

Figure 3. Differences in the Standards of Care Required of Financial Planners.

## Consumers May Not Understand That Financial Planners Have Potential Conflicts of Interest When Selling Products

As seen in figure 3, financial planners are subject to different standards of care in their capacities as investment advisers, broker-dealers, and insurance agents.

- *Fiduciary Standard of Care*: As noted earlier, investment advisers are subject to a fiduciary standard of care—that is, they must act in their client's best interest, ensure that recommended investments are suitable for the client, and disclose to the client any material conflicts of interest.[32] According to SEC and NASAA representatives, the fiduciary standard applies even when investment advisers provide advice or recommendations about products other than securities, such as insurance, in conjunction with advice about securities.
- *Suitability Standard of Care When Recommending Security Products*: FINRA regulation requires broker-dealers to adhere to a suitability standard when rendering investment recommendations—that is, they must recommend only those securities that they reasonably believe are suitable for the customer.[33] Unlike the fiduciary standard, suitability rules do not necessarily require that the client's best interest be served. According to FINRA staff, up-front general disclosure of a broker-dealer's business activities and relationships that may cause conflicts of interest is not required.[34] However, according to SEC, broker-dealers are subject to many FINRA rules that require disclosure of conflicts in certain situations, although SEC staff also note that those rules may not cover every possible conflict of interest, and disclosure may occur after conflicted advice has already been given.[35]
- *Suitability Standard of Care When Recommending Insurance Products*: Standards of care for the recommendation and sale of insurance products vary by product and by state. For example, as seen earlier, NAIC's model regulations on the suitability standard for annuity transactions, adopted by some states but not others, require consideration of the insurance needs and financial objectives of the customer, while NAIC's model regulation for life insurance does not include a suitability requirement *per se*.

Conflicts of interest can exist when, for example, a financial services professional earns a commission on a product sold to a client. Under the fiduciary standard applicable to investment advisers, financial planners must mitigate any potential conflicts of interest and disclose any that remain. But under a suitability standard applicable to broker-dealers, conflicts of interest may exist and generally may not need to be disclosed up-front.[36] For example, as confirmed by FINRA, financial planners functioning as broker-dealers may recommend a product that provides them with a higher commission than a similar product with a lower commission, as long as the product is suitable and the broker-dealer complies with other requirements. Because the same individual or firm can offer a variety of services to a client—a practice sometimes referred to as "hat switching"—these services could be subject to different standards of care. As such, representatives of consumer groups and others have expressed concern that consumers may not fully understand which standard of care, if any, applies to a financial professional. As shown above, the standards of care—and the extent to which conflicts of interest must be disclosed—can vary depending on the capacity in which the individual serves.[37] A 2007 report by the Financial Planning Association stated that "it would be difficult, if not impossible, for an individual investor to discern when the adviser was acting in a fiduciary capacity or in a non-fiduciary capacity."[38] A 2008 SEC study conducted by the RAND Corporation, consisting of a national household survey and six focus group discussions with investors, found that consumers generally did not understand not only the distinction between a suitability and fiduciary standard of care but also the differences between broker-dealers and investment advisers.[39] Similarly, a 2010 national study of investors found that most were confused about which financial professionals are required to operate under a fiduciary standard that requires professionals to put their client's interest ahead of their own.[40]

Representatives of financial services firms that provide financial planning told us they believe that clients are sufficiently informed about the differing roles and accompanying standards of care that a firm representative may have. They noted that when they provide both advisory and transactional services to the same customer, each service—such as planning, brokerage, or insurance sales—is accompanied by a separate contract or agreement with the customer. These agreements disclose that the firm's representatives have different obligations to the customer depending on their role. In addition, once a financial plan has been provided, some companies told us that they have customers sign an additional agreement stating that the financial planning relationship with the firm has ended.

Recent revisions by SEC to Form ADV disclosure requirements were designed to address, among other things, consumer understanding of potential conflicts of interest by investment advisers and their representatives. Effective October 12, 2010, SEC revised Form ADV, Part 2, which financial service firms must provide to new and prospective clients.[41] The new form, which must be written in plain English, is intended to help consumers better understand the activities and affiliations of their investment adviser. It requires additional disclosures about a firm's conflicts of interest, compensation, business activities, and disciplinary information that is material to an evaluation of the adviser's integrity. Similarly, in October 2010 FINRA issued a regulatory notice requesting comments on a concept proposal regarding possible new disclosure requirements that would, among other things, detail for consumers in plain English the conflicts of interest that broker-dealers may have associated with their services.[42]

Section 913 of the Dodd-Frank Act requires SEC to study the substantive differences between the applicable standards of care for broker-dealers and investment advisers; the effectiveness of the existing legal or regulatory standards of care for brokers, dealers, and investment advisers; and consumers' ability to understand the different standards of care. SEC will also consider the potential impact on retail customers of imposing the same fiduciary standard that now applies to investment advisers on broker-dealers when they provide personalized investment advice. Under the act, SEC may promulgate rules to address these issues and is specifically authorized to establish a uniform fiduciary duty for broker-dealers and investment advisers that provide personalized investment advice about securities to customers. As a result, further clarification of these standards may be forthcoming. FINRA officials told us that they support a fiduciary standard of care for broker-dealers when they provide personalized investment advice to retail customers.

Consumer confusion on standards of care may also be a source of concern with regard to the sale of some insurance products. A 2010 national survey of investors found that 60 percent mistakenly believed that insurance agents had a fiduciary duty to their clients.[43] Some insurance products, such as annuities, are complex and can be difficult to understand, and annuity sales practices have drawn complaints from consumers and various regulatory actions from state regulators as well as SEC and FINRA for many years.[44] According to NAIC, many states have requirements that insurance salespersons sell annuities only if the product is suitable for the customer. However, NAIC notes that some states do not have a suitability requirement for annuities. Consumer groups and others have stated that high sales commissions on certain insurance products, including annuities, may provide salespersons with a substantial financial incentive to sell these products, which may or may not be in the consumer's best interest. As a result of section 989J of the Dodd-Frank Act, one type of annuity—the indexed annuity—is to be regulated by states as an insurance product, rather than regulated by SEC as a security, under certain conditions.[45]

SEC's pending study related to the applicable standards of care for broker-dealers and investment advisers will not look at issues of insurance that fall outside of SEC's jurisdiction. NAIC has not undertaken a similar study regarding consumer understanding of the standard of care for insurance agents. As we reported in the past, financial markets function best when consumers understand how financial service providers and products work and know how to choose among them.[46] Given the evidence of consumer confusion about differing standards of care and given the increased risks that certain insurance products can pose, there could be benefits to an NAIC review of consumers' understanding of standards of care for high-risk insurance products.

## Consumers May be Confused about the Ways Financial Professionals Present Themselves to the Public

Individuals who provide financial planning services may use a variety of titles when presenting themselves to the public, including financial planner, financial consultant, and financial adviser, among many others. However, evidence suggests that the different titles financial professionals use can be confusing to consumers. The 2008 RAND study found that even experienced investors were confused about the titles used by broker-dealers and investment advisers, including financial planner and financial adviser. Similarly, in consumer focus groups of investors conducted by SEC in 2005 as part of a rulemaking process, participants were generally unclear about the distinctions among titles, including broker, investment adviser, and financial planner.[47] In addition, a representative of one consumer advocacy group has expressed concern that some financial professionals may use as a marketing tool titles suggesting that they provide financial planning services, when in fact they are only selling products. One industry group, the Financial Planning Coalition, also has noted that some individuals may hold themselves out as financial planners without meeting minimum training or ethical requirements. Federal and state regulators told us they generally focused their oversight and enforcement actions on financial planners' activities rather than the titles they use. Moreover, NASAA has said that no matter what title financial planners use, most are required to register as investment adviser representatives and must satisfy certain competency requirements, including passing an examination or obtaining a recognized professional designation.[48]

Financial planners' professional designations are typically conferred by a professional or trade organization. These designations may indicate that a planner has passed an examination, met certain educational requirements, or had related professional experience. Some of these designations require extensive classroom training and examination requirements and include codes of ethics with the ability to remove the designation in the event of violations. State securities regulators view five specific designations as meeting or exceeding the registration requirements for investment adviser representatives, according to NASAA, and allow these professional designations to satisfy necessary competency requirements for prospective investment adviser representatives.[49] For example, one of these five designations requires a bachelor's degree from an accredited college or university, 3 years of full-time personal financial planning experience, a certification examination, and 30 hours of continuing education every 2 years.

The criteria used by organizations that grant professional designations for financial professionals vary greatly. FINRA has stated that while some designations require formal certification procedures, including examinations and continuing professional education credits, others may merely signify that membership dues have been paid. The Financial Planning Coalition and The American College, a nonprofit educational institution that confers several financial designations, similarly told us that privately conferred designations range from those with rigorous competency, practice, and ethical standards and enforcement to those that can be obtained with minimal effort and no ongoing evaluation.

As noted earlier, designations that imply expertise or special training in advising senior citizen or elderly investors have received particular attention from regulators. A joint report of SEC, FINRA, and NASAA described cases in which financial professionals targeted seniors by using senior-specific designations that implied that they had a particular expertise for senior investors, when in fact they did not; as noted earlier, NASAA and NAIC have developed a model rule to address the issue.[50] The report also noted these professionals targeted seniors through the use of so-called free-lunch seminars, where free meals are offered in exchange for attendance of a financial education seminar. However, the focus of the seminars was actually on the sale of products rather than the provision of financial advice.

Given the large number of designations financial planners may use, concerns exist that consumers may have difficulty distinguishing among them. To alleviate customer confusion, FINRA has developed a Web site for consumers that provides the required qualifications and other information about the designations used by securities professionals. The site lists more than 100 professional designations, 5 of which include the term “financial planner,” and 24 of which contain comparable terms such as financial consultant or counselor.[51] The American College told us that it had identified 270 financial services designations. Officials from NASAA, NAIC, and a consumer advocacy organization told us that consumers might have difficulty distinguishing among the various designations. Officials from The American College told us that the number of designations itself was not necessarily a cause for concern, but rather consumers’ broadly held misperception that all designations or credentials are equal.

To help address these concerns, FINRA plans to expand its Web site on professional designations to include several dozen additional designations related to insurance. However, FINRA officials noted that consumers’ use of this tool has been limited. For example, in 2009, the site received only 55,765 visits. A recent national study of the financial capability of American adults sponsored by FINRA found that only 15 percent of adults who had used a financial professional in the last 5 years claimed to have checked the background, registration, or license of a financial professional.[52] In addition, SEC staff acknowledged that there have been concerns about confusing designations, and SEC’s October 2010 changes to investment adviser disclosure requirements mandate that investment adviser representatives who list professional designations and certifications in their background information also provide the qualifications needed for these designations, so that the consumer can understand the value of the designation for the services being provided.

Section 917 of the Dodd-Frank Act includes a requirement that SEC conduct a study identifying the existing level of financial literacy among retail investors, including the most useful and understandable relevant information that they need to make informed financial decisions before engaging a financial intermediary. While the section does not specifically mention the issue of financial planners’ titles and designations, the confusion we found to exist could potentially be addressed or mitigated if SEC incorporated this issue into its overall review of financial literacy among investors. SEC staff told us that at this time its review would not likely address this issue, although it would address such things as the need for conducting background checks on financial professionals. Financial markets function best when consumers have information sufficient to understand and assess financial service providers and products.[53] Including financial planners' use of titles and designations in SEC's financial literacy review could provide useful information on the implications of consumers' confusion on this issue.

## Consumer Complaints and Enforcements Actions Appear to be Relatively Limited, but Regulators Generally Do Not Track Data Specific to Financial Planners

Available data do not show a large number of consumer complaints and enforcement actions involving financial planners, but the exact extent to which financial planners may be a source of problems is unknown. We were able to find limited information on consumer complaints from various agencies. For example, representatives of FTC and the Better Business Bureau said that they had received relatively few complaints related to financial planners. FTC staff told us that a search in its Consumer Sentinel Network database for the phrase "financial planner" found 141 complaints in the 5-year period from 2005 through 2010 but that only a handful of these appeared to actually involve activity connected to the financial planning profession.[54] The staff added that additional searches on other titles possibly used by financial planners, such as financial consultant and personal financial adviser, did not yield significant additional complaints. In addition, a representative of the Better Business Bureau told us that it had received relatively few complaints related to financial planners, although the representative noted that additional complaints might exist in broader categories, such as "financial services."

Consumer complaint data may not be an accurate gauge of the extent of problems. Complaints may represent only a small portion of potential problems and complaints related to "financial planners" may not always be recorded as such. As we have previously reported, consumers also may not always know where they can report complaints.[55] At the same time, some complaints that are made may not always be valid.

SEC has limited information on the extent to which the activities of financial planners may be causing consumers harm. The agency does record and track whether federally and state-registered investment adviser firms provide financial planning services, but its data tracking systems for complaints, examination results, and enforcement actions are not programmed to readily determine and track whether the complaint, result, or action was specifically related to a financial planner or financial planning service. For example, SEC staff told us the number of complaints about financial planners would be undercounted in their data system that receives and tracks public inquiries, known as the Investor Response Information System, because this code would likely be used only if it could not be identified whether the person (or firm) was an investment adviser or broker-dealer. In addition, the data system that SEC uses to record examination results, known as the Super Tracking and Reporting System, does not allow the agency to identify and extract examination results specific to the financial planning services of investment advisers.

However, SEC staff told us that a review of its Investor Response Information System identified 51 complaints or inquiries that had been recorded using their code for issues related to "financial planners" between November 2009 and October 2010. SEC staff told us that the complaints most often involved allegations of unsuitable investments or fraud, such as misappropriation of funds.[56] A review of a separate SEC database called Tips, Complaints, and Referrals—an interim system that was implemented in March 2010—found 124 allegations of problems possibly related to financial planners from March 2010 to October 2010.[57]

SEC staff told us that they did not have comprehensive data on the extent of enforcement activities related to financial planners *per se*. In addition, NASAA said that states generally do not track enforcement data specific to financial planners. At our request, SEC and NASAA provided us with examples of enforcement actions related to individuals who held themselves out as financial planners. Using a keyword search, SEC identified 10 such formal enforcement actions between August 2009 and August 2010. According to SEC documents, these cases involved allegations of such activities as defrauding clients through marketing schemes, receiving kickbacks without making proper disclosures, and misappropriation of client funds. Although NASAA also did not have comprehensive data on enforcement activities involving financial planners, representatives provided us with examples of 36 actions brought by 30 states from 1986 to 2010. These cases involved allegations of such things as the sale of unsuitable products, fraudulent misrepresentation of qualifications, failure to register as an investment adviser, and misuse of client funds for personal expenses.

Because of limitations in how data are gathered and tracked, SEC and state securities regulators are not currently able to readily determine the extent to which financial planning services may be causing consumers harm. NASAA officials told us that, as with SEC, state securities regulators did not typically or routinely track potential problems specific to financial planners. SEC and NASAA representatives told us that they had been meeting periodically in recent months to prepare for the transition from federal to state oversight of certain additional investment adviser firms, as mandated under the Dodd-Frank Act, but they said that oversight of financial planners in particular had not been part of these discussions. SEC staff have noted that additional tracking could consume staff time and other resources. They also said that because there are no laws that directly require registration, recordkeeping, and other responsibilities of "financial planners" *per se*, tracking such findings relating to those entities would require expenditure of resources on something that SEC does not have direct responsibility to oversee. Yet as we have reported in the past, while we recognize the need to balance the cost of data collection efforts against the usefulness of the data, a regulatory system should have data sufficient to identify risks and problem areas and support decisionmaking.[58] Given the significant growth in the financial planning industry, ongoing concerns about potential conflicts of interest, and consumer confusion about standards of care, regulators may benefit from identifying ways to get better information on the extent of problems specifically involving financial planners and financial planning services.

## Some Changes in the Oversight of Financial Planners Could be Beneficial, but Most Stakeholders Believe Substantial Overhaul Is Not Needed

### Stakeholders Have Suggested a Variety of Approaches to the Regulation of Financial Planners

Over the past few years, a number of stakeholders—including consumer groups, FINRA, and trade associations representing financial planners, securities firms, and insurance firms—have proposed different approaches to the regulation of financial planners. Following are four of the most prominent approaches, each of which has both advantages and disadvantages.

***Creation of a Board to Oversee Financial Planners***

In 2009, the Financial Planning Coalition—comprised of the Certified Financial Planner Board of Standards, Financial Planning Association, and the National Association of Personal Financial Advisors—proposed that Congress establish a professional standards-setting oversight board for financial planners. According to the coalition, its proposed legislation would establish federal regulation of financial planners by allowing SEC to recognize a financial planner oversight board that would set professional standards for and oversee the activities of individual financial planners, although not financial planning firms. For example, the board would have the authority to establish baseline competency standards in the areas of education, examination, and continuing education, and would be required to establish ethical standards designed to prevent fraudulent and manipulative acts and practices. It would also have the authority to require registration or licensing of financial planners and to perform investigative and disciplinary actions. Under the proposal, states would retain antifraud authority over financial planners as well as full oversight for financial planners' investment advisory activity. However, states would not be allowed to impose additional licensing or registration requirements for financial planners or set separate standards of conduct. Supporters of a new oversight board have noted that its structure and governance would be analogous to the Public Company Accounting Oversight Board, a private nonprofit organization subject to SEC oversight that in turn oversees the audits of public companies that are subject to securities laws. According to the Financial Planning Coalition, a potential advantage of this approach is that it would treat financial planning as a distinct profession and would regulate across the full spectrum of activities in which financial planners may engage, including activities related to investments, taxes, education, retirement planning, estate planning, insurance, and household budgeting. Proponents argue that a financial planning oversight board would also help ensure high standards and consistent regulation for all financial planners by establishing common standards for competency, professional practices, and ethics.

However, many securities regulators and financial services trade associations with whom we spoke said that they believe such a board would overlap with and in many ways duplicate existing state and federal regulations, which already cover virtually all of the products and services that a financial planner provides. Some added that the board would entail unnecessary additional financial costs and administrative burdens for the government and regulated entities. In addition, some opponents of this approach question whether "financial planning" should be thought of as a distinct profession that requires its own regulatory structure, noting that financial planning is not easily defined and can span multiple professions, including accounting, insurance, investment advice, and law. One consumer group also noted that the regulation of individuals and professions is typically a state rather than a federal responsibility. Finally, we note that the analogy to the Public Company Accounting Oversight Board may not be apt. That board was created in response to a crisis involving high-profile bankruptcies and investor losses caused in part by inadequacies among public accounting firms. In the case of financial planners, there is limited evidence of an analogous crisis or, as noted earlier, of severe harm to consumers.

***Augmenting Oversight of Investment Advisers with an SRO***

A number of proposals over the years have considered having FINRA or a newly created SRO supplement SEC oversight of investment advisers. These proposals date back to at least 1963, when an SEC study recommended that all registered investment advisers be required to be a member of an SRO.[59] In 1986, the National Association of Securities Dealers, a predecessor to FINRA, explored the feasibility of examining the investment advisory activities of members who were also registered as investment advisers. The House of Representatives passed a bill in 1993 that would have amended the Advisers Act to authorize the creation of an "inspection only" SRO for investment advisers, although the bill did not become law.[60] In 2003, SEC requested comments on whether one or more SROs should be established for investment advisers, citing, among other reasons, concerns that the agency's own resources were inadequate to address the growing numbers of advisers.[61] However, SEC did not take further action. Section 914 of the Dodd-Frank Act required SEC to issue a study in January 2011 on the extent to which one or more SROs for investment advisers would improve the frequency of examinations of investment advisers.[62]

According to FINRA, the primary advantage of augmenting investment adviser oversight with an SRO is that doing so would allow for more frequent examinations, given the limited resources of states and SEC. The Financial Services Institute, an advocacy organization for independent broker-dealers and financial advisers, has stated that an industry-funded SRO with the resources necessary to appropriately supervise and examine all investment advisers would close the gap that exists between the regulation of broker-dealers and investment advisers. FINRA said that it finds this gap troubling given the overlap between the two groups (approximately 88 percent of all registered advisory representatives are also broker-dealer representatives). FINRA adds that any SRO should operate subject to strong SEC oversight and that releasing SEC of some of its responsibilities for investment advisers would free up SEC resources for other regulatory activities.

However, NASAA, some state securities regulators, and one academic with whom we spoke opposed adding an SRO component to the regulatory authority of investment advisers. NASAA said it believed that investment adviser regulation is a governmental function that should not be outsourced to a private, third-party organization that lacks the objectivity, independence, expertise, and experience of a government regulator. Further, NASAA said it is concerned with the lack of transparency associated with regulation by SROs because, unlike government regulators, they are not subject to open records laws through which the investing public can obtain information. Two public interest groups, including the Consumer Federation of America, have asserted that one SRO—FINRA—has an "industry mindset" that has not always put consumer protection at the forefront. In addition, the Investment Adviser Association and two other organizations we interviewed have noted that funding an SRO and complying with its rules can impose additional costs on a firm.[63]

### *Extending Coverage of the Fiduciary Standard*

Proposals have been made to extend coverage of the fiduciary standard of care to all those who provide financial planning services. Some consumer groups and others have stated that a fiduciary standard should apply to anyone who provides personalized investment advice about securities to retail customers, including insurance agents who recommend securities. The Financial Planning Coalition has proposed that the fiduciary standard apply to all those who hold themselves out as financial planners. Proponents of extending the fiduciary standard of care, which also include consumer groups and NASAA, generally maintain that consumers should be able to expect that financial professionals they work with will act in their best interests. They say that a fiduciary standard is more protective of consumers' interests than a suitability standard, which requires only that a product be suitable for a consumer rather than in the consumer's best interest. In addition, the Financial Planning Coalition notes that extending a fiduciary standard would somewhat reduce consumer confusion about financial planners that are covered by the fiduciary standard in some capacities (such as providing investment advice) but not in others (such as selling a product).

However, some participants in the insurance and broker-dealer industries have argued that a fiduciary standard of care is vague and undefined. They say that replacing a suitability standard with a fiduciary standard could actually weaken consumer protections since the suitability of a product is easier to define and enforce. Opponents also have argued that complying with a fiduciary standard would increase compliance costs that in turn would be passed along to consumers or otherwise lead to fewer consumer choices.

### *Clarifying Financial Planners' Credentials and Standards*

The American College has proposed clarifying the credentials and standards of financial professionals, including financial planners. In particular, it has proposed creating a working group of existing academic and practice experts to establish voluntary credentialing standards for financial professionals. As noted previously, consumers may be unable to distinguish among the various financial planning designations that exist and may not understand the requirements that underpin them. Clarifying the credentials and standards of financial professionals could conceivably take the form of prohibiting the use of certain designations, as has been done for senior-specific designations in some states, or establishing minimum education, testing, or work experience requirements needed to obtain a designation. The American College has stated that greater oversight of such credentials and standards could provide a "seal of approval" that would generally raise the quality and competence of financial professionals, including financial planners, help consumers distinguish among the various credentials, and help screen out less qualified or reputable players.

However, the ultimate effectiveness of such an approach is not clear, since the extent to which consumers take designations into account when selecting or working with financial planners is unknown, as is the extent of the harm caused by misleading designations. In addition, implementation and ongoing monitoring of financial planners' credentials and standards could be challenging. Further, the issue of unclear designations has already been addressed to some extent—for example, as noted earlier, some states regulate the use of certain senior-specific designations and allow five professional designations to satisfy necessary competency requirements for prospective investment adviser representatives. State securities regulators also have the authority to pursue the misleading use of credentials through their existing antifraud authority.

### Most Stakeholders Saw Little Need for an Additional Oversight Body Governing Financial Planners

In general, a majority of the regulatory agencies, consumer groups, academics, trade associations, and individual financial services companies with which we spoke did not favor substantial structural change in the regulation of financial planners. In particular, few supported an additional oversight body, which was generally seen as duplicative of existing regulation. Some stakeholders in the securities and insurance industries noted that given the dynamic financial regulatory environment under way as a result of the Dodd-Frank Act—such as creation of a new Bureau of Consumer Financial Protection—more time should pass before additional regulatory changes related to financial planning services were considered. Several industry associations also noted that opportunities existed for greater enforcement of existing law and regulation, as discussed earlier.

## CONCLUSION

Existing statutes and regulations appear to cover the great majority of financial planning services, and individual financial planners nearly always fall under one or more regulatory regimes, depending on their activities. While no single law governs the broad array of activities in which financial planners may engage, given available information, it does not appear that an additional layer of regulation specific to financial planners is warranted at this time. At the same time, as we have previously reported, more robust enforcement of existing laws could strengthen oversight efforts. In addition, there are some actions that can be taken that may help address consumer protection issues associated with the oversight of financial planners.

First, as we have reported, financial markets function best when consumers understand how financial providers and products work and know how to choose among them. Yet consumers may be unclear about standards of care that apply to financial professionals, particularly when the same individual or firm offers multiple services that have differing standards of care. As such, consumers may not always know whether and when a financial planner is required to serve their best interest. While SEC is currently addressing the issue of whether the fiduciary standard of care should be extended to broker-dealers when they provide personalized investment advice about securities, the agency is not addressing whether this extension should also apply to insurance agents, who generally fall outside of SEC's jurisdiction. Sales practices involving some high-risk insurance products, such as annuities, have drawn attention from federal and state regulators. A review by NAIC of consumers' understanding of the standards of care with regard to the sale of insurance products could provide information on the extent of consumer confusion in the area and actions needed to address the issue.

Second, we have seen that financial planners can adopt a variety of titles and designations. The different designations can imply different types of qualifications, but consumers may not understand or distinguish among these designations, and thus may be unable to properly assess the qualifications and expertise of financial planners. SEC's recent changes in this area—requiring investment advisers to disclose additional information on professional designations and certifications they list—should prove beneficial. Another opportunity lies in SEC's mandated review of financial literacy among investors. Incorporating issues of consumer confusion about financial planners' titles and designations into that review could assist the agency in assessing whether any further changes are needed in disclosure requirements or other related areas.

Finally, SEC has limited information about the nature and extent of problems specifically related to financial planners because it does not track complaints, examination results, and enforcement activities associated with financial planners specifically, and distinct from investment advisers as a whole. However, a regulatory system should have data sufficient to identify risks and problem areas and support decisionmaking. SEC staff have noted that additional tracking could require additional resources, but other opportunities may also exist to gather additional information on financial planners. Because financial planning is a growing industry and has raised certain consumer protection issues, regulators could potentially benefit from better information on the extent of problems specifically involving financial planners and financial planning services.

## Recommendations

We recommend that the National Association of Insurance Commissioners, in concert with state insurance regulators, take steps to assess consumers' understanding of the standards of care with regard to the sale of insurance products, such as annuities, and take actions as appropriate to address problems revealed in this assessment.

We also recommend that the Chairman of the Securities and Exchange Commission direct the Office of Investor Education and Advocacy, Office of Compliance Inspections and Examinations, Division of Enforcement, and other offices, as appropriate, to:

- Incorporate into SEC's ongoing review of financial literacy among investors an assessment of the extent to which investors understand the titles and designations used by financial planners and any implications a lack of understanding may have for consumers' investment decisions; and
- Collaborate with state securities regulators in identifying methods to better understand the extent of problems specifically involving financial planners and financial planning services, and take actions to address any problems that are identified.

## Agency Comments

We provided a draft of this report for review and comment to FINRA, NAIC, NASAA, and SEC. These organizations provided technical comments, which we incorporated, as appropriate. In addition, NAIC provided a written response. NAIC said it generally agreed with the contents of the draft report and would give consideration to our recommendation regarding consumers' understanding of the standards of care with regard to the sale of insurance products.

NASAA also provided a written response. In its response, NASAA said it agreed that a specific layer of regulation for financial planners was unnecessary and provided additional information on some aspects of state oversight of investment advisers. NASAA also said that it welcomed the opportunity to continue to collaborate with SEC to identify methods to better understand and address problems specifically involving financial planners, as we recommended. In addition, NASAA expanded upon the reasons for its opposition to proposals that would augment oversight of investment advisers with an SRO.

Alicia Puente Cackley
Director, Financial Markets and Community Investment

## APPENDIX I. SCOPE AND METHODOLOGY

Our reporting objectives were to address (1) how financial planners are regulated and overseen at the federal and state levels, (2) what is known about the effectiveness of regulation of financial planners and what regulatory gaps or overlap may exist, and (3) alternative approaches for the regulation of financial planners and the advantages and disadvantages of these approaches.

For background information, we obtained estimates for 2000 and 2008, and projections for 2018, from the Bureau of Labor Statistics on the number of individuals who reported themselves as "personal financial advisers," a term that the agency said was interchangeable with "financial planner." The bureau derived these estimates from the Occupational Employment Statistics survey and the Current Population Survey.[64] According to the bureau, the Occupational Employment Statistics' estimates for financial planners have a relative standard error of 1.9 percent, and the median wage estimate for May 2009 has a relative standard error of 1.5 percent. Because the overall employment estimates used are developed from multiple surveys, it was not feasible for the bureau to provide the relative standard errors for these financial planner employment statistics. To estimate the number of households that used financial planners, we analyzed 2007 data from the Board of Governors of the Federal Reserve's Survey of Consumer Finances. This survey is conducted every three years to provide detailed information on the finances of U.S. households.[65] Because the survey is a probability sample based on random selections, the sample is only one of a large number of samples that might have been drawn. Since each sample could have provided different estimates, we express our confidence in the precision of our particular sample's results as a 95 percent confidence interval (e.g., plus or minus 2.5 percentage points). This is the interval that would contain the actual population value for 95 percent of the samples that could have been drawn. In this report, for this survey, all percentage estimates have 95 percent confidence intervals that are within plus or minus 2.5 percentage points from the estimate itself.

To identify how financial planners are regulated and overseen at the federal and state levels, we identified and reviewed, on the federal level, federal laws, regulations, and guidance applicable to financial planners, the activities in which they engage, and their marketing materials, titles, and designations. We also reviewed relevant SEC interpretive releases, such as IA Rel. No. 1092, *Applicability of the Investment Advisers Act to Financial Planners, Pension Consultants, and Other Persons Who Provide Investment Advisory Services as a Component of Other Financial Services*. We also discussed the laws and regulations relevant to financial planners in meetings with staff of the Securities and Exchange Commission (SEC), Financial Industry Regulatory Authority (FINRA), Department of Labor, and Internal Revenue Service. We also interviewed two legal experts and reviewed a legal compendium on the regulation of financial planners. At the state level, we interviewed representatives from the North American Securities Administrators Association (NASAA) and the National Association of Insurance Commissioners (NAIC) and reviewed model regulations developed by these agencies. In addition, we selected five states—California, Illinois, North Carolina, Pennsylvania, and Texas—for a more detailed review. We chose these states because they had a large number of registered investment advisers and varying approaches to the regulation of financial planners, and represented geographic diversity. For each of these states, we reviewed selected laws and regulations related to financial planners, which included those related to senior-specific designations and insurance transactions, and we interviewed staff at each state's securities and insurance agencies.

To identify what is known about the effectiveness of the regulation of financial planners and what regulatory gaps or overlap may exist, we reviewed relevant federal and state laws, regulations and guidance. In addition, we spoke with representatives of the federal and state agencies cited above, as well as FINRA and organizations that represent or train financial planners, including the Financial Planning Coalition, The American College, and the CFA Institute; organizations that represent the financial services industry, including the Financial Services Institute, Financial Services Roundtable, Securities Industry and Financial Markets Association, Investment Advisers Association, American Society of Pension & Professional Actuaries, National Association of Insurance and Financial Advisors, American Council of Life Insurers, Association for Advanced Life Underwriting, American Institute of

Certified Public Accountants, American Bankers Association; and organizations representing consumer interests, including the Consumer Federation of America and AARP. We also spoke with selected academic experts knowledgeable about these issues. In addition, we reviewed relevant studies and other documentary evidence, including a 2008 study of the RAND Corporation that was commissioned by SEC, "Investor and Industry Perspectives on Investment Advisers and Broker-Dealers"; "Results of Investor Focus Group Interviews About Proposed Brokerage Account Disclosures," sponsored by SEC; results of the FPA Fiduciary Task Force, "Final Report on Financial Planner Standards of Conduct"; "U.S. Investors & The Fiduciary Standard: A National Opinion Survey," sponsored by AARP, the Consumer Federation of America, the NASAA, the Investment Adviser Association, the Certified Financial Planner Board of Standards, the Financial Planning Association, and the National Association of Personal Financial Advisors; and the 2009 National Financial Capability Study, commissioned by FINRA. We determined that the reliability of these studies was sufficient for our purposes. In addition, we reviewed relevant information on the titles and designations used by financial planners, including FINRA's Web site that provides the required qualifications and other information about the designations used by securities professionals.

We also obtained and reviewed available data on complaints and selected enforcement actions related to financial planners from the Federal Trade Commission, Better Business Bureau, and SEC. We collected from the Federal Trade Commission complaint data from its Consumer Sentinel Network database, using a keyword search of the term "financial planner" for complaints filed from 2005 to 2010. From the Better Business Bureau, we collected the number of complaints about the financial planning industry received in 2009. From SEC, we collected complaints from the agency's Investor Response Information System that had been coded as relating to "financial planners" from November 2009 to October 2010. We also reviewed data from SEC's Tips, Complaints, and Referrals database that resulted from a keyword search for the terms "financial planner," "financial adviser," "financial advisor," "financial consultant," and "financial counselor" from March 2010 to October 2010. In addition, at our request, SEC and NASAA provided us anecdotally with examples of enforcement actions related to individuals who held themselves out as financial planners. SEC identified 10 formal enforcement actions between August 2009 and August 2010 and NASAA provided us selected examples of state enforcement actions involving financial planners from 1986 to 2010 from 30 states. We gathered information on SEC- and state-registered investment advisers from SEC's Investment Adviser Registration Database. FINRA did not provide us with data on complaints, examination results, or enforcement actions specific to financial planners; FINRA officials told us they do not track these data specific to financial planners.

To identify alternative approaches for the regulation of financial planners and their advantages and disadvantages, we conducted a search for legislative and regulatory proposals related to financial planners, which have been made by Members of Congress, consumer groups, and representatives of the financial planning, securities, and insurance industries. We identified and reviewed position papers, studies, public comment letters, congressional testimonies, and other documentary sources that address the advantages and disadvantages of these approaches. In addition, we solicited views on these approaches from representatives of the wide range of organizations listed above, including organizations that represent financial planners, financial services companies, and consumers, as well as state and federal government agencies and associations and selected academic experts.

We conducted this performance audit from June 2010 through January 2011 in accordance with generally accepted government auditing standards. Those standards require that we plan and perform the audit to obtain sufficient, appropriate evidence to provide a reasonable basis for our findings and conclusions based on our audit objectives. We believe that the evidence obtained provides a reasonable basis for our findings and conclusions based on our audit objectives.

## End Notes

[1] While the Bureau of Labor Statistics reports these statistics using the term "financial adviser," bureau officials said that this term could be used interchangeably with financial planner. The bureau broadly defined a "personal financial adviser" as an individual who provides financial planning services and that private bankers or wealth managers would also be categorized as financial advisers.

[2] Our percentage estimates based on the 2007 Survey of Consumer Finances have 95 percent confidence intervals of +/- 2.5 percentage points or less. For example, we are 95 percent confident that between 8.2 and 11.8 percent of households in the bottom quartile used financial planners for investment decisions. See appendix I for additional information.

[3] Investment Adviser Act Release No. 1092, 52 Fed. Reg. 38400, 38401 (Oct. 16, 1987) (IA Rel. No. 1092).

[4] The Advisers Act defines an investment adviser as any person (i.e., individual or firm) who is in the business of providing advice, or issuing reports or analyses, regarding securities, for compensation. 15 U.S.C. § 80b-2(a)(11); IA Rel. No. 1092. In addition to applicable securities law, investment advice related to a retirement savings plan, such as a 401(k) plan,

may also be subject to the Employee Retirement Income Security Act. The requirements under that act are outside the scope of this study. A forthcoming GAO report, GAO-11-119, will provide more information on investment advice in 401(k) plans.

[5] In *SEC v. Capital Gains Research Bureau, Inc.*, 375 U.S. 180, 189-192 (1963), the U.S. Supreme Court recognized that the Advisers Act imposes a fiduciary duty on investment advisers. This standard imposes an affirmative duty to act solely in the best interests of the client. The investment adviser also must eliminate or disclose all conflicts of interest.

[6] 15 U.S.C. § 80b-3a. The term investment adviser can refer to a person or firm. Investment adviser firms generally register with SEC or state securities departments as registered investment advisers. According to NASAA, certain natural persons that are employed by firms generally register with the state securities departments as investment adviser representatives.

[7] *Id.* Under 17 C.F.R. § 275.203A-1, SEC registration has been optional for certain investment advisers having assets under management between $25 and $30 million. Firms also may have a different basis for registering with SEC (other than the amount of client assets the firm has under management), such as whether the principal office and place of business are within a state that has no registration requirement.

[8] Pub. L. No. 111-203, § 410, 124 Stat. 1376, 1576-77 (2010).

[9] In registering with SEC or a state, investment adviser firms are required to report whether they provide financial planning services in Part 1A of the Uniform Application for Investment Adviser Registration, Item 5 G(1). SEC does not provide a definition of financial planning services for firms to use when completing the registration form. The total number of investment adviser firms overseen—including both those that do and do not provide financial planning services—is 15,016 for the states and 11,873 for SEC. For data on investment adviser firms, firms that were registered with both SEC and the states were counted with SEC-registered investment adviser firms.

[10] See 75 Fed. Reg. 77052 (Dec. 10, 2010) (SEC proposed rule, which, if finalized, would give advisers until August 20, 2011, to report the market value of their assets under management to the SEC as the first step in the process).

[11] GAO, *Securities and Exchange Commission: Steps Being Taken to Make Examination Program More Risk-Based and Transparent*, GAO-07-1053 (Washington, D.C.: Aug. 14, 2007). As we noted, since the detection of mutual fund trading abuses in late 2003, in light of limited resources, SEC has shifted its approach to examinations of investment advisers from one that focused on routinely examining all registered firms, regardless of risk, to one that focuses on more frequently examining those firms and industry practices at higher risk for compliance issues.

[12] GAO. SEC reported in February 2010 that it is now placing a greater emphasis on fraud detection, in addition to identifying potential violations of securities laws and rules, strengthening procedures and internal controls to maximize limited resources, recruiting examiners with specialized skills, and increasing expertise through enhanced training.

[13] According to NASAA, New York, Minnesota, and Wyoming do not register investment adviser representatives, although New York and Minnesota do have certain examination and other requirements that must be met.

[14] The brokerage and insurance services provided by these investment adviser firms are not necessarily a part of their financial planning services. In addition, many financial planners may sell securities- or insurance-related products through affiliated brokers or agents.

[15] The primary law for regulating broker-dealers is the Securities Exchange Act of 1934, codified at 15 U.S.C. §§ 78a-78oo. Brokers effect transactions for the account of others, while dealers buy and sell securities for their own accounts. 15 U.S.C. § 78c. The term registered representative is generally used to refer to certain employees of a broker-dealer firm who are engaged in providing securities recommendations. Broker-dealers must be members of a qualifying self-regulatory organization (either a national exchange or a registered securities association). 15 U.S.C. § 78o(b)(8).

[16] Under NASD Conduct Rule 2310, a FINRA member making an investment recommendation to a customer must have grounds for believing that the recommendation is suitable for that customer's financial situation and needs. In November 2010, SEC approved FINRA's proposed new consolidated rules governing the suitability obligations of its members. 75 Fed. Reg. 71479 (Nov. 23, 2010). This rule, proposed FINRA Rule 2111, requires salespersons to have a reasonable basis for believing, based on adequate due diligence, that a recommendation of a transaction or strategy is suitable for at least some investors; that the recommendation is suitable for a specific customer, based on that customer's profile; and that a series of recommended transactions is not excessive and unsuitable for the customer.

[17] NAIC amended this model regulation in March 2010; according to NAIC, one state has adopted the updated model and additional states are expected to do so.

[18] According to NAIC, in 4 of these 32 states the regulation applies only when the consumers are senior citizens.

[19] NASD Notice to Members 96-86 outlines that variable contracts for insurance products are subject to suitability requirements.

[20] NASD Interpretive Material 2210-2 outlines guidance concerning communications with the public about variable life insurance and variable annuities. FINRA has proposed that this guidance be replaced by a separate new FINRA Rule 2211. See FINRA Rule Filing No. SR-FINRA-2009-070.

[21] GAO, *Insurance Reciprocity and Uniformity: NAIC and State Regulators Have Made Progress in Producer Licensing, Product Approval and Market Conduct Regulation, but Challenges Remain*, GAO-09-372 (Washington, D.C.: Apr. 6, 2009). Reciprocity refers to the extent to which state regulators accept other states' regulatory actions. Uniformity refers to the extent to which states have implemented either the same, or substantially similar, regulatory standards and procedures.

[22] 17 C.F.R. § 275.206(4)-1.

[23] NASD Rule 2210.

[24] SEC and the states use Form ADV to register investment adviser firms and collect information from them. Part 2 of Form ADV provides information about the investment adviser and its business for use of the clients and is publicly available on the Investment Adviser Public Depository Web site. The SEC adopted amendments to Form ADV that were effective October 12, 2010, requiring Part 2 of Form ADV be written in a plain English narrative format. *See* Amendments to Form ADV, 75 Fed. Reg. 49,234 (Aug. 12, 2010) (to be codified at 17 C.F.R. pt. 275 and 279).

[25] The District of Columbia and Puerto Rico also include financial planners in their definitions of investment adviser, according to NASAA.

[26] GAO, *Life Insurance Settlements: Regulatory Inconsistencies May Pose a Number of Challenges*, GAO-10-775 (Washington, D.C.: July 9, 2010).

[27] Section 1011 of the Dodd-Frank Act established the Bureau of Consumer Financial Protection to regulate "the offering and provision of consumer financial products or services under the Federal consumer financial laws." A financial product or service is defined in section 1002(15)(A)(viii) of the act to include financial advisory services to consumers on individual financial matters, with the exception of advisory services related to securities provided by a person regulated by SEC or a state securities commission to the extent that such person acts in a regulated capacity. Accordingly, it appears that the bureau may have jurisdiction over financial planners to the extent that they may offer services that would not be under the jurisdiction of SEC or a state securities commission.

[28] The members of this coalition include the Certified Financial Planner Board of Standards, Inc.; the Financial Planning Association; and the National Association of Personal Financial Advisors.

[29] 15 U.S.C. § 80b-2(a)(11); IA Rel. No. 1092(II)(B), at 38403. Under 15 U.S.C. § 80b-2(a)(11)(C), brokers and dealers also cannot receive any special compensation for their services in order to be exempt from registration as an investment adviser.

[30] *Id.*

[31] *Id.* The Advisers Act excludes bank and bank holding companies from the definition of investment adviser. Further, a bank and a bank holding company is an investment adviser under the act to the extent that the bank or bank holding company serves or acts as an adviser to a registered investment company. If such services are performed in a separate department or division of a bank, the department or division and not the bank itself is the investment adviser.

[32] The SEC has, in effect, established rules of conduct for investment advisers, including requirements for disclosing conflicts of interest, obtaining the best execution on behalf of clients, allocating investments among clients fairly, ensuring that investments are suitable for clients, and ensuring that there is a reasonable basis for recommendations. SEC also requires investment advisers to maintain records pertaining to client accounts and business operations.

[33] A broker-dealer must have an adequate and reasonable basis for any recommendation and must make recommendations based on a customer's financial situation, needs and other securities holdings.

[34] Letter from Marc Menchel, Executive Vice President and General Counsel, FINRA, to Elizabeth M. Murphy, Secretary, SEC 4 (Aug. 25, 2010), available at http://www.finra.org/web/groups/industry/@ip/@reg/@guide/documents/industry/p121983.pdf.

[35] The standards of conduct for broker-dealers may also be based on antifraud provisions of the securities law and agency principles. Broker-dealers also have a duty of fairness in their contracts with a customer, which requires them to disclose material information that the customer would consider important as an investor. In addition, broker-dealers that handle discretionary accounts are generally thought to owe fiduciary obligations to their customers.

[36] FINRA officials have stated that they believe that the regulation of broker-dealers—while lacking an express fiduciary duty—prescribes in great detail the conduct and supervision of broker-dealers who provide investment advice to retail customers.

[37] Black's Law Dictionary (9th ed. 2009) defines the term "conflict of interest" as a "real or seeming incompatibility between one's private interests and one's public or fiduciary duties."

[38] *Final Report on Financial Planner Standards of Conduct*, FPA Fiduciary Task Force, June 2007.

[39] Angela A. Hung et al., RAND Institute for Civil Justice, *Investor and Industry Perspectives on Investment Advisers and Broker-Dealers* (2008).

[40] Infogroup, Opinion Research Corporation, *U.S. Investors & The Fiduciary Standard: A National Opinion Survey*, September 15, 2010. The survey was conducted among a sample of 2,012 adults living in the continental United States, including 1,319 who identified themselves as investors. The survey was sponsored by AARP, the Consumer Federation of America, NASAA, the Investment Adviser Association, the Certified Financial Planner Board of Standards, the Financial Planning Association, and the National Association of Personal Financial Advisors.

[41] Amendments to Form ADV, 75 Fed. Reg. 49234 (Aug. 12, 2010) (requires investment advisers registered with SEC to provide new and prospective clients with a brochure and brochure supplements clearly setting forth a meaningful, current disclosure of the business practices, conflicts of interest and background of the investment adviser and its advisory personnel; and requires the brochures to be filed with SEC electronically, which will make them available to the public through its Web site).

[42] FINRA Regulatory Notice 10-54.

[43] Infogroup, Opinion Research Corporation, *U.S. Investors & The Fiduciary Standard: A National Opinion Survey*, September 15, 2010.

[44] See, for example, Securities and Exchange Commission Rule 151A and Annuities: Issues and Legislation, CRS Report for Congress 7-7500 (July 29, 2010).

[45] State regulation applies so long as a state has adopted NAIC's Suitability in Annuity Transactions model regulation or if an insurance company adopts and implements practices on a nationwide basis that meet or exceed the minimum requirements established by NAIC's model regulation. Indexed annuities are products that guarantee a purchaser's principal and a certain rate of return, and offer a chance for additional returns linked to a securities index or indices.

[46] GAO, *Financial Regulation: A Framework for Crafting and Assessing Proposals to Modernize the Outdated U.S. Financial Regulatory System*, GAO-09-216 (Washington, D.C.: Jan. 8, 2009).

[47] *Results of Investor Focus Group Interviews About Proposed Brokerage Account Disclosures.* Report to the Securities and Exchange Commission by Siegel & Gale LLC and Gelb Consulting Group, Inc., Mar. 10, 2005.

[48] According to NASAA, all but three states—New York, Minnesota, and Wyoming—register investment adviser representatives and require that they pass either the Series 65 (Uniform Investment Adviser Law Examination) or the Series 66 (Uniform Combined State Law Examination), or obtain a recognized professional designation. While New York and Minnesota do not register individual investment adviser representatives, their state laws require that the representatives meet other requirements, such as passing certain examinations or obtaining a professional designation accepted by the state.

[49] The five designations recognized as such are Certified Financial Planner®, Chartered Financial Consultant®, Personal Financial Specialist, Chartered Financial Analyst, and Chartered Investment Counselor.

[50] *Protecting Senior Investors: Report of Examinations of Securities Firms Providing "Free Lunch" Sales Seminars* by the Office of Compliance Inspections and Examination, Securities and Exchange Commission; North American Securities Administrators Association; and the Financial Industry Regulatory Authority, September 2007.

[51] See http://apps.finra.org/DataDirectory/1/prodesignations.aspx .

[52] Applied Research & Consulting LLC, *Financial Capability in the United States: Initial Report of the Research Findings from the 2009 National Survey*, prepared for the FINRA Investor Education Foundation (New York: December 2009).

[53] GAO.

[54] The Consumer Sentinel Network database is a secure online database of millions of consumer complaints available only to law enforcement. In addition to storing complaints received by FTC, the Consumer Sentinel Network also includes complaints filed with the Internet Crime Complaint Center, Better Business Bureaus, Canada's PhoneBusters, the U.S. Postal Inspection Service, the Identity Theft Assistance Center, and the National Fraud Information Center, among others.

[55] GAO, *Telecommunications: FCC Needs to Improve Oversight of Wireless Phone Service*, GAO-10-34 (Washington, D.C.: November 2009), p. 18.

[56] Of these 51 complaints or inquiries, 29 involved allegations of fraud, 9 involved allegations of unsuitable investments, and the remaining 13 represented questions on a variety of topics.

[57] Of these 124 allegations, 13 were coded as "fraudulent or unregistered offer or sale of securities, including Ponzi schemes, high yield investment programs or other investment programs"; 12 as "manipulation of a security's price or volume"; 6 as "theft or misappropriation of funds or securities"; 5 as "false or misleading statements about a company"; 3 as "problems with my brokerage or advisory account"; and 2 as "insider trading." An additional 14 were coded as "other fraudulent conduct" and 69 were coded simply as "other."

[58] GAO, *Managing for Results, Using GPRA to Help Congressional Decisionmaking and Strengthen Oversight*, GAO/T-00-95 (Washington, D.C.: March 2000), p. 13. GAO, *Executive Guide, Effectively Implementing the Government Performance and Results Act*, GAO/GGD-96-118 (Washington, D.C.: June 1996), p. 27.

[59] See Securities and Exchange Commission, News Digest Issue No. 63-4-3, 8 (1963), which describes SEC's report to Congress, regarding the adequacy of the rules of national securities exchanges and national securities associations, pursuant to Pub. L. No. 87-196, 75 Stat. 465 (1961), wherein SEC points out that the framework of industry self-regulation permitted many broker-dealer firms and registered investment advisers to remain outside of any official self-regulatory group. According to the SEC News Digest, the report suggested that membership in an SRO should be a prerequisite to registration with SEC as a broker-dealer or investment adviser.

[60] H.R. 578, 103rd Cong. (1993).

[61] Investment Advisers Act Release No. 2107, 68 Fed. Reg. 7038 (Feb. 11, 2003).

[62] SEC is required to report the results of its study within 180 days of enactment of the Dodd-Frank Act.

[63] The Investment Adviser Association is a not-for-profit association that represents the interests of SEC-registered investment adviser firms.

[64] As explained by the Bureau of Labor Statistics, the Occupational Employment Statistics program produces employment and wage estimates for over 800 occupations. These are estimates of the number of people employed in certain occupations, and estimates of the wages paid to them. Since self-employed persons are not included in the estimates, the bureau also considers information from the Current Population Survey, a monthly survey of households conducted by the Bureau of Census for the Bureau of Labor Statistics, to derive its occupation estimates.

[65] Additional information on the sample design and data collected by the Survey of Consumer Finances is available at http://www.federalreserve.gov/pubs/oss/oss2/about.html.

In: Financial Planners, Investment Advisers ... ISBN: 978-1-62257-837-5
Editors: T. Davis and G. S. Crawford 

*Chapter 2*

# STUDY AND RECOMMENDATIONS ON IMPROVED INVESTOR ACCESS TO REGISTRATION INFORMATION ABOUT INVESTMENT ADVISERS AND BROKER-DEALERS*

*U.S. Securities and Exchange Commission*

## I. INTRODUCTION

### A. The Congressional Mandate

The Dodd-Frank Wall Street Reform and Consumer Protection Act (the "Dodd-Frank Act" or "Act") was signed into law on July 21, 2010.[1] Section 919B of the Act directs the Securities and Exchange Commission (the "Commission" or "SEC") to complete a study, including recommendations, of ways to improve the access of investors to registration information about registered and previously registered investment advisers, associated persons of investment advisers,[2] brokers and dealers and their associated persons,[3] and to identify additional information that should be made publicly available. The

* This is an edited, reformatted and augmented version of the U.S. Securities and Exchange Commission, As Required by Section 919B of the Dodd-Frank Wall Street Reform and Consumer Protection Act, dated January 2011.

Act specifies that the study include an analysis of the advantages and disadvantages of further centralizing access to registration information, and identify data pertinent to investors and the method and format for displaying and publishing the data to enhance the information's accessibility and utility to investors. The Act requires the Commission to complete the study within six months after the date of enactment of the Act (*i.e.*, by January 21, 2011), and to implement any recommendations within eighteen months after completion of the study.

## B. Organization of the Study

The Commission's Office of Investor Education and Advocacy ("OIEA") prepared the study in consultation with the Division of Investment Management, the Division of Trading and Markets, the Division of Risk, Strategy, and Financial Innovation, and the Office of the General Counsel (collectively, the "Staff").[4] OIEA also sought input from the Financial Industry Regulatory Authority, Inc. ("FINRA"), an industry self-regulatory organization ("SRO"), and the North American Securities Administrators Association ("NASAA").[5] The study does not necessarily reflect the views of the Commission or the individual Commissioners. The study was approved for release by the Commission.[6]

The study is organized into eight sections. Following this introductory section, Section II provides an executive summary of the study. Section III contains an overview of the registration information the Staff believes is important to investors, as well as a brief introduction to the primary sources of publicly available registration information. Section IV discusses broker-dealer registration and disclosure, including a history of the Central Registration Depository ("CRD") and BrokerCheck.[7] Section IV also discusses the registration information available through BrokerCheck, as well as the format and usage of BrokerCheck. Section V discusses investment adviser registration and disclosure, including a history of the Investment Adviser Registration Depository ("IARD") and Investment Adviser Public Disclosure ("IAPD"), the public disclosure arm of IARD.[8] Section V also discusses the type of registration information available through IAPD, as well as IAPD format and usage. Section VI compares the nature of information available in BrokerCheck and IAPD.

Section VII proposes several recommendations. For the near-term, *i.e.*, within the eighteen-month implementation period, the Staff makes the following recommendations: (1) unify search returns for BrokerCheck and IAPD to help investors more easily obtain the data they need to make informed decisions regarding financial services providers; (2) add a search by ZIP code or other indicator of location to BrokerCheck and IAPD to increase the utility of the existing databases; and (3) enhance BrokerCheck and IAPD by adding educational content to make the data currently available more useful to investors.

The Staff also recommends that, subsequent to the eighteen-month implementation period, Commission staff and FINRA continue to analyze, including through investor testing, the feasibility and advisability of expanding BrokerCheck to include information currently available in CRD, as well as the method and format of publishing that information; and that Commission staff continue to evaluate expanding IAPD content and the method and format of publishing that content, including through investor testing. Section VIII concludes the study.

## II. EXECUTIVE SUMMARY

This study responds to Section 919B of the Dodd-Frank Act, which mandates that the Commission study ways to improve the access of investors to registration information about investment advisers and broker-dealers, including analyzing the advantages and disadvantages of further centralizing access to registration information contained in CRD and IARD.

The Commission and its staff have long maintained that investors should examine relevant registration information before choosing a broker-dealer or investment adviser.[9] Information pertaining to a broker-dealer or investment adviser's federal or state registration, such as information about its associated persons, including licensing and other qualification data, disciplinary and employment history, contact information, and customer complaints, can help investors make better-educated decisions in selecting a broker-dealer or investment adviser, as well as better protect themselves against fraud.

Currently, a significant amount of registration data is publicly available, primarily through BrokerCheck (for broker-dealers and their associated persons who are registered) and IAPD (for investment advisers and their associated persons). Additionally, both the Commission and state securities regulators require investment advisers to deliver to advisory clients brochures and brochure supplements regarding employees, including investment adviser representatives, who provide advisory services.[10] State securities regulators also act as an important source of registration information about broker-dealers, certain investment advisers, and their associated persons. This study provides the background and history of both BrokerCheck and IAPD and describes the data publicly available on each system.

While the current process enables investors to obtain registration information about a broker-dealer or investment adviser, improvements could be made within the statutorily-mandated eighteen-month period that would further promote investors' interests. In that context, the Staff makes a number of recommendations. First, the Staff, pursuant to Section 919B, considered the advantages and disadvantages of further centralizing the two systems. The primary advantage would be to provide investors access to relevant data through one request, regardless of whether they seek data about a broker-dealer or an investment adviser. The Staff believes that a unified public disclosure database would be optimal to achieve this goal. However, the practical difficulties involved – including Section 919B's eighteen-month timeframe for implementation – militate toward a near-term recommendation that would involve less structural change. As a result, the study recommends unifying search returns for BrokerCheck and IAPD while continuing to maintain the separate databases. This would allow investors to find registration information on both broker-dealers and investment advisers, regardless of whether investors are using BrokerCheck or IAPD.

Second, the study includes two additional recommendations pertaining to increasing the usefulness of the systems to investors. The Staff recommends that BrokerCheck and IAPD search functions be expanded to permit searches for broker-dealers, investment advisers, registered representatives, and investment adviser representatives, based on ZIP code or other indicator of location. This feature would offer a valuable tool for investors who are beginning a search for a broker-dealer, investment adviser, or registered person, but who have limited online access to registration data organized by location. The Staff further recommends that BrokerCheck and IAPD be enhanced by adding educational content, such as links and definitional material, perhaps, embedded in alternate text tags (*e.g.*, "bubbles," "pop-ups," or other kinds of "hover" text) that would appear automatically whenever a user's electronic cursor hovers over certain text or items on the BrokerCheck and IAPD Web pages. These functions would provide definitions or other explanatory content to help a user better understand the significance of a particular technical term or reference. Both Forms BD and ADV contain a glossary of terms that could be used to populate the hover text.

The Staff also recommends that, subsequent to the eighteen-month implementation period, Commission staff and FINRA continue to analyze, including through investor testing, the feasibility and advisability of expanding BrokerCheck to include information currently available in CRD, as well as the method and format of publishing that information; and that Commission staff continue to evaluate expanding IAPD content and the method and format of publishing that content, including through investor testing. Potential modifications could include adding summary data for advisory firms on IAPD, hyperlinks between CRD numbers and SEC file numbers containing information related to a particular CRD number, and additional links to content available elsewhere on BrokerCheck or IAPD.

# III. Background: Registration Information Pertinent to Investors and an Overview of Sources of Publicly-Available Data

## A. Registration Information Pertinent to Investors

Because selecting a broker-dealer or investment adviser is one of the most important decisions that investors face, information to help them make this choice should be easy to find, easy to use, and easy to understand. The Commission recognizes that "[i]nvestors are entrusting registered representatives with their savings and should have sufficient pertinent information available to enable them to select a registered representative with whose background they are comfortable."[11] Accordingly, the Commission has recommended that the investing public use all available sources of information to conduct thorough searches of any associated person's activities.[12]

OIEA encourages investors to evaluate thoroughly the background of any broker-dealer or investment adviser that they use or plan to engage. Significant aspects of OIEA's investor education and outreach program are based on the premise that investors can better avoid fraud and potential investment losses if they gather pertinent data before engaging a broker-dealer or investment adviser.[13] The information that the Commission believes is important for investors to consider in their decision-making is described in a series of OIEA publications, including *Invest Wisely: Advice from Your Securities Regulators,*[14] *Ask Questions,*[15] and *Protect Your Money: Check Out Brokers and Investment Advisers.*[16] These educational and outreach materials, that can be requested directly from financial firms or from federal or state regulators, describe various types of information that investors should consider, including:

- the registration status of the firm and its representatives with state or federal regulators;
- basic information about the firm and its representatives, including the primary place of business, formal business address, and contact information;
- a listing and description of the licenses held by the financial services provider, such as a series 7, 65, or 66, and the dates of passage of those examinations by registered representatives;
- descriptions of the credentials of investment advisers and financial planners;
- the educational background of registered persons;
- recent employment history of registered persons, particularly details about tenure with financial firms with a focus on the frequency of job changes or changes in the names of firms they represent;
- the disciplinary record of the firm and the registered person;
- a description of current and historic arbitrations, complaints, or litigation by clients against a firm or registered person;
- Form ADV for registered investment advisers;
- a description of the scope and type of investment services offered by the broker-dealer or investment adviser;
- a description of fees and compensation arrangements describing the manner and the nature of the work for which broker-dealers, investment advisers, and their associated persons are compensated; and
- for broker-dealers, a description of whether the broker-dealer and its clearing firm are members of the Securities Investor Protection Corporation.

## B. Access to BrokerCheck and IAPD

BrokerCheck and IAPD are Web-based disclosure systems that provide investors with access to the information described above. These databases help investors to investigate and evaluate broker-dealers, registered representatives, investment advisers, and investment adviser representatives. The Commission has stated that it "recognizes that the public's ability to access information" through BrokerCheck, "whether to inquire about a registered person or formerly associated person, may serve to protect investors, the integrity of the marketplace, and the public interest."[17] Similarly, the Commission has noted that IAPD "allows the public to access the most recent Form ADV filing made by an investment adviser,"[18] that a "client may use this disclosure [on Form ADV] to select his or her own adviser and evaluate the adviser's business practices and conflicts on an ongoing basis," and that "the disclosure clients and prospective clients receive is critical to their ability to make an informed decision about whether to engage an adviser and, having engaged the adviser, to manage that relationship."[19]

Both BrokerCheck and IAPD can be accessed from the Commission's Web page at http://www.sec.gov/investor/brokers.htm. In addition, investors can access BrokerCheck at http://brokercheck.finra.org, through FINRA's main Web page at http://www.finra.org, and through FINRA's investor education foundation Web site at http://www.finrafoundation.org/resources. Investors can access IAPD at www.adviserinfo.sec.gov. Further, the OIEA-maintained investor education Web site, www.Investor.gov, provides links to both BrokerCheck and IAPD, and several OIEA investor education publications and outreach materials reference those Web sites as well.

## C. Overview of Sources of Publicly-Available Data Regarding Broker-Dealers, Investment Advisers, and Their Associated Persons

There is no single source of registration information regarding U.S. broker-dealers, investment advisers, and their associated persons. This reflects the fact that broker-dealers and investment advisers are regulated under two different regulatory regimes, with oversight shared among federal and state securities regulators and FINRA. The Commission has regulatory authority over broker-dealers, investment advisers that are required to register with the Commission, and their associated persons.[20] Broker-dealers register with the Commission and the states in which they do business, and must also become members of an SRO, which, in most cases, is FINRA. A broker-dealer's registered representatives ("registered representatives") do not register with the Commission, but with the states in which they do business and with FINRA.

The Commission regulates large advisory firms exclusively, while smaller advisory firms are overseen by the states in which they do business.[21] The dividing line between larger and smaller advisory firms is based on the amount of assets managed by the investment adviser and currently stands at $25 million.[22] Pursuant to an amendment to the Advisers Act and a Commission rule proposal, beginning July 21, 2011, investment advisers with assets under management ("AUM") of over $100 million must register with the Commission, while investment advisers with less than $100 million in AUM register only with the states.[23]

Investment adviser representatives, like registered representatives, do not register with the Commission. Investment adviser representatives register only with the states. There is no SRO for investment advisers or investment adviser representatives. Advisory firms and their representatives may, however, be dually registered as broker-dealers and investment advisers or as registered representatives and investment adviser representatives. Fewer than 20% of registered broker-dealers were also registered as an investment adviser in 2010,[24] and approximately 5% of SEC-registered advisory firms were registered as broker-dealers.[25] However, the approximately 611 firms dually registered with the Commission generally constitute very large firms in terms of assets and number of employees.[26] As a result, most investment adviser representatives also are registered representatives. Of the approximately 275,675 investment adviser representatives identified in IAPD in October 2010, approximately 87.5% were registered as both investment adviser representatives and registered representatives, either for the same firm or multiple firms.[27]

Reflecting the differences in regulatory regimes, broker-dealers, investment advisers, and registered representatives and investment adviser representatives register using two separate systems. CRD, which is operated by FINRA, is the repository of registration and disciplinary information regarding broker-dealers and registered representatives. Electronic public access to certain CRD data is available through FINRA's BrokerCheck Web site. FINRA maintains control over the data in those systems, as well as the design, functionality, and output of the BrokerCheck Web site.

IARD, which is owned by the Commission and operated by FINRA, is the repository of registration and disciplinary information about investment advisers and investment adviser representatives. Electronic public access to the information filed through IARD is available on the IAPD Web site. FINRA operates IARD and IAPD under contract with the Commission.

States use CRD to register broker-dealers and registered representatives doing business in their state; and states register the investment advisers and investment adviser representatives they oversee, as required by state law, typically through IARD.[28] States generally do not post broker-dealer or investment adviser registration records on their Web sites, but many provide links to BrokerCheck and IAPD, and provide investors with copies of CRD records and IARD records upon request, on paper or electronically.[29]

# IV. Broker-Dealer Registration and Disclosure

## A. History of CRD and BrokerCheck

Generally, brokers, who are engaged in the business of buying and selling securities for their customers' accounts, and dealers, who are engaged in the business of buying and selling securities for their own account, are regulated under the Securities Exchange Act of 1934 (the "Exchange Act").[30] Congress amended the Exchange Act in 1938 to allow for private sector oversight of brokers and dealers, commonly referred to as self-regulation, which led to the creation of the National Association of Securities Dealers ("NASD"), now known as FINRA.[31] FINRA developed the CRD database in conjunction with NASAA to centralize registration for the broker-dealer industry.[32] When implemented in 1981, CRD consolidated a multi-state, paper-based registration process into a single, nationwide filing process and computer system.[33] Information in CRD is obtained through forms (the "Uniform Forms") that registered representatives, broker-dealers, and regulators complete as part of the securities industry registration and licensing process. Six different Uniform Forms are used to file information with CRD: (i) Form U4 (Uniform Application for Securities Industry Registration or Transfer); (ii) Form U5 (Uniform Termination Notice for Securities Industry Registration); (iii) Form U6 (Uniform Disciplinary Action Reporting Form); (iv) Form BD (Uniform Application for Broker-Dealer Registration), a Commission form; (v) Form BDW (Uniform Request for Broker-Dealer Withdrawal), also a Commission form; and (vi) Form BR (Uniform Branch Office Registration Form).[34]

In 1988, FINRA established the Public Disclosure Program, the predecessor of BrokerCheck, to provide the public with information on the professional background, business practices, and conduct of FINRA members and their associated persons.[35] In 1998, Internet access to registration data became available when FINRA began to provide public access to members' registration information and their associated persons' employment history through its Web site.[36] In 1999, FINRA introduced "Web CRD," which allowed the electronic filing of registration forms through its Web site.[37] By 2002, more than 95% of the public inquiries to the Public Disclosure Program were received through the Internet.[38] In response to this demand, FINRA proposed establishing a central electronic gateway to information about broker-dealers, which led to the creation of BrokerCheck, whose primary purpose is to help investors make informed choices about the individuals and firms with which they may wish to do business.[39] In 2006, Congress required FINRA to establish and maintain a system for collecting and maintaining registration information and a readily accessible electronic process to receive and respond to inquiries about registration information, as well as adopt rules governing such inquiries and the type and scope of information to be provided in response.[40]

## B. Data Available on BrokerCheck

BrokerCheck provides public access to certain CRD registration data about broker-dealers and registered representatives.[41] The information on BrokerCheck regarding registered representatives is derived from the information on the Uniform Forms, including Forms BD, BDW, U4, U5, U6, and BR. Information on formerly registered representatives is available for ten years after de-registration, and permanently for registered representatives who were the subject of a final regulatory action.[42]

FINRA Rule 8312 governs the information that FINRA releases to the public regarding broker-dealers and registered representatives and requires them to keep their registration data accurate and up-to-date.[43] The rule has been revised several times in the past decade to increase the amount and type of information available to the public on BrokerCheck. For example, FINRA amended the rule in 2000 to continue to provide records about former registered representatives for two years after their association with a member firm had been terminated.[44] In 2007, the Commission approved FINRA's amendment to Rule 8312 to provide for disclosure of examinations passed by registered representatives. FINRA also amended Rule 8312 to expand disclosure of arbitration awards to include those awards that historically were not reported because they fell below a specified dollar amount.[45] These rule amendments established a threshold for publicly disclosing "historic" customer complaints at least two years old that either remained unresolved or settled for less than a specified dollar amount.[46]

In 2009, the Commission approved FINRA's amendment to Rule 8312 to make available permanently in BrokerCheck information about former registered representatives who were the subject of a final regulatory action, such as an action brought by a federal, state, or foreign financial regulatory authority, or an SRO.[47] Effective November 2010, the Commission approved FINRA's amendment to Rule 8312 to make BrokerCheck reports on former registered representatives publicly available for ten years after association with a member firm.[48] Previously, BrokerCheck reports on former registered representatives were made publicly available for only two years following their exit from the industry.[49]

Also in 2010, the Commission approved FINRA's amendment to Rule 8312 to expand the information regarding former registered representatives that is available permanently on BrokerCheck.[50] Prior to these amendments, criminal convictions and civil injunctions in connection with investment-related activities were disclosed for a two-year period following the termination of a registered representative's association with a member firm. Following the 2010 amendments, that information is disclosed permanently.[51] The 2010 amendments also made "historic" customer complaints publicly available through BrokerCheck in every case. Prior to those amendments, historic complaints were made publicly available through BrokerCheck only where: (i) they became historic complaints on or after March 19, 2007; (ii) the most recent historic complaint was less than ten years old; and (iii) the registered representative had a total of three or more disclosable regulatory actions, currently reported customer complaints, arbitrations, or litigations.[52]

Pursuant to the current version of FINRA Rule 8312, BrokerCheck provides the following information (subject to certain exceptions for personal and other information as set forth in the rule)[53] with respect to current and former members, current associated persons, and persons associated with a member in the preceding ten years:

- any information reported on the most recently filed Form U4, Form U5, Form U6, Form BD, and Form BDW;
- currently approved registrations;
- summary information about certain arbitration awards against a member involving a securities or commodities dispute with a public customer;
- the most recently submitted comment, if any, provided to FINRA by the person who is covered by BrokerCheck, in the form and in accordance with the procedures established by FINRA, for inclusion

with the information provided through BrokerCheck (only comments that relate to the information provided through BrokerCheck are included);

- information as to qualification examinations passed by the person and date passed (FINRA does not release information regarding examination scores or failed examinations);
- in response to telephonic inquiries via the BrokerCheck toll-free telephone listing, whether a particular member is subject to the provisions of NASD Rule 3010 (b)(2) (FINRA's taping rule);
- historic complaints (*i.e.*, the information last reported on Uniform Forms relating to customer complaints that are more than two years old and that have not been settled or adjudicated, and customer complaints, arbitrations or litigations that have been settled for an amount less than $10,000 prior to May 18, 2009 or an amount less than $15,000 on or after May 18, 2009 and are no longer reported on a Uniform Form), provided that any such matter became a Historic Complaint on or after August 16, 1999; and
- the name and succession history for current or former members.[54]

In addition, BrokerCheck provides the following information (subject to certain exceptions for personal and other information as set forth in the rule)[55] with respect to persons who were formerly associated with a member, but who have not been associated with a member within the preceding ten years, and (A) were ever the subject of a final regulatory action as defined in Form U4 that has been reported to CRD on a Uniform Form; or (B) were registered with FINRA on or after August 16, 1999, and any of the following applies, as reported to CRD on a Uniform Form: (i) was convicted of or pled guilty or *nolo contendere* to a crime; (ii) was the subject of a civil injunction in connection with investment-related activity or a civil court finding of involvement in a violation of any investment-related statute or regulation; or (iii) was named as a respondent or defendant in an investment-related, consumer-initiated arbitration or civil litigation which alleged that the person was involved in a sales practice violation and which resulted in an arbitration award or civil judgment against the person:

- information regarding the event(s) enumerated above or as reported on a Uniform Form;

- administrative information, including employment history and registration history derived from information reported on a Uniform Form;
- the most recently submitted comment, if any, provided to FINRA by the person who is covered by BrokerCheck, in the form and in accordance with the procedures established by FINRA, for inclusion with the information provided through BrokerCheck (only comments that relate to the information provided through BrokerCheck are included); and
- information as to qualifications examinations passed by the person and date passed (FINRA does not release information regarding examination scores or failed examinations).[56]

Not all information in CRD is disclosed to the public through BrokerCheck. The following CRD information is not made publicly available on BrokerCheck:

- *Reasons and Comments Related to Termination.* In situations where a broker-dealer terminates a registered representative, BrokerCheck reports exclude the reason for the termination and any comments from the former registered representative regarding the termination, although this information is reported on Form U5. FINRA also excludes from BrokerCheck, generally, information on Form U4 for registered representatives who have terminated registration more than ten years ago.[57]
- *Formerly Reportable Information.* Certain information that was, but is no longer required to be, reported through the registration and licensing process is not disclosed through BrokerCheck. This information includes, for example, judgments and liens originally reported as outstanding that have been satisfied and bankruptcy proceedings filed more than ten years ago.
- *Examination Details.* Scores on industry qualification examinations, and failed examinations, are also excluded from BrokerCheck reports, although BrokerCheck displays industry examinations that a registered representative has passed.[58]
- *Previous Filings.* BrokerCheck provides only the most recent filings by broker-dealers and their associated persons; it does not provide access to previous filings.

- *Discretionary Disclosure.* FINRA, on a case-by-case basis, reserves the right to exclude information that contains confidential customer information, offensive or potentially defamatory language or information that raises significant identity theft or privacy concerns that are not outweighed by investor protection concerns. Also, in certain limited circumstances, FINRA's policy allows for information to be expunged from CRD, most often pursuant to a court order.
- *Personal Information.* FINRA does not include Social Security numbers, home addresses, or physical descriptions in BrokerCheck reports.
- *Certain Criminal Charges.* Criminal charges that did not result in convictions and certain other actions that did not lead to an award or finding against the registered representative, for whatever reason, are not disclosed through BrokerCheck.

## C. BrokerCheck Format and Usage

BrokerCheck's format allows users to search by name or registration number for a registered representative or broker-dealer. Results are displayed in a one-page summary; more detailed information is available as well. An investor who accesses BrokerCheck seeking information about a broker-dealer would be presented with the following information in the heading for the summary report: the name of the firm; its registration number or numbers; the address of its main office; its mailing address; and its business telephone number. An investor who accesses BrokerCheck for information on an individual registered representative would be presented with the following information in the heading for the summary report: the name of the individual; the individual's registration number; the name and address of the firm with which the individual is currently employed and registered; and the length of time the individual has been registered with that firm.

In 1999, a year after FINRA began making records available on its Web site, FINRA received more than one million inquiries, and by 2002, it was fielding more than two million inquiries a year.[59] Usage has increased since BrokerCheck was deployed in March 2007. More than 20 million searches were conducted on the BrokerCheck Web site in 2009, with approximately 18.5 million summary records viewed and approximately 3.8 million requests for detailed reports on a registered representative or a broker-dealer.[60] However, FINRA is unable to determine the number of unique visitors to

BrokerCheck because BrokerCheck does not use persistent "cookies" – small data files that would allow it to recognize repeat visitors. FINRA is further unable to identify the percentage of visitors to the BrokerCheck Web site that are individual investors, regulators, or brokerage industry members.[61]

# V. INVESTMENT ADVISER REGISTRATION AND DISCLOSURE

## A. History of IARD and IAPD

Investment advisers receive compensation for providing advice to others about investing in securities.[62] Investment advisers use Form ADV under the Investment Advisers Act of 1940 ("Advisers Act") to apply for registration with the Commission or with state securities authorities.[63] The Commission adopted Form ADV in 1954 and has amended the form several times since then.[64] For example, in 1985, the Commission, together with NASAA, developed a new version of Form ADV – the "Uniform Application for Investment Adviser Registration" – to serve as the investment adviser registration form for all jurisdictions requiring registration.[65] This uniform Form ADV is the basis of the form that investment advisers use today.[66]

Amendments to Form ADV in 1979 promulgated the so-called "brochure rule" that currently requires certain investment advisers subject to registration with the Commission under the Advisers Act to furnish clients and prospective clients with a written document – the brochure – and one or more brochure supplements, containing the information required by Part 2 of Form ADV.[67] The brochure rule requires investment advisers to deliver the brochure directly to clients and prospective clients before or at the time of entering into an investment advisory contract, and each year thereafter to provide clients with either (i) a copy of the current (updated) brochure, or (ii) a summary of material changes to the brochure that includes an offer to provide a copy of the current brochure.[68] The Commission recently changed the presentation requirements of the brochure from a check-the-box type format to a narrative format designed to provide investors with clearly written, meaningful, current disclosure of the business practices, conflicts of interest, and background of the investment adviser.[69]

Currently, investment advisers subject to registration under the Advisers Act are required to file Form ADV (including the Part 2A brochure – but not the Part 2B brochure supplement)[70] electronically through IARD. Prior to 1996, most investment advisers were required to register with the Commission as well as with each state in which they did business, using paper-based forms. The National Securities Market Improvement Act of 1996 ("NSMIA") eliminated this system of dual registration and consolidated oversight.[71] In most cases, NSMIA mandated that oversight of larger advisory firms be left exclusively to the Commission, with smaller firms to be overseen by the states in which they do business.[72] Under NSMIA, the dividing line was based on the amount of assets managed by the adviser, and was set at $25 million.[73] Under the Dodd-Frank Act, that threshold will rise to $100 million on July 21, 2011.[74]

NSMIA also authorized the Commission to establish an electronic filing system for investment advisers, to require advisers to pay the costs associated with the system, and to provide investors with a readily accessible database of information about investment advisers.[75] Under this authority, the Commission adopted a rule in 2000 requiring advisers to register electronically by filing through IARD, starting in 2001.[76] The Commission contracted with FINRA to operate IARD, citing its technical expertise in running Web CRD.[77] FINRA continues to operate IARD under contract with the Commission. The Commission, in consultation with the state securities authorities with respect to Uniform Forms, retains decision-making authority with respect to expanding IARD and the information that is collected by this system. The Commission recently has adopted a significant revision to the core information collection documents for investment advisers,[78] and is preparing to implement additional changes to the investment adviser registration regime pursuant to the Dodd-Frank Act.[79]

IAPD has been in operation since 2001 for investment advisory firms. IAPD displays records for SEC- and state-registered advisers, and was expanded in mid-2010 to include investment adviser representatives.[80] IAPD also contains information on formerly registered advisers and investment adviser representatives. In November 2010, the system was modified to retain information about advisory firms and investment adviser representatives that de-registered in the past ten years, mirroring changes, approved a few months earlier, to BrokerCheck for former registered representatives.[81] Previously, IAPD displayed data on advisory firms for two years after their de-registration.

In the second half of 2010, there were approximately 11,889 SEC-registered investment advisers and approximately 14,688 state registered investment advisers on IAPD.[82] The Staff anticipates that approximately 4,100 SEC-registered advisers will shift to state oversight once the Dodd-Frank

Act's higher threshold for SEC oversight of advisers takes effect on July 21, 2011. A Dodd-Frank Act requirement for registration of certain private investment fund managers is expected to add approximately 750 SEC-registered advisers, for a net reduction of approximately 3,350 SEC-registered advisers.

## B. Data Available on IARD and IAPD

Although IARD was modeled on CRD,[83] the systems differ in design to accommodate the fact that advisory firms register using different forms than broker-dealers. The investment adviser forms that are on IAPD are Form ADV and Form ADV-E.[84] Investment adviser representative information on IAPD is summarized from various state sources, including:

- Forms U4, U5, and U6;
- current registration status and effective date of investment adviser representative registrations from IARD and/or CRD;
- investment adviser representative comments submitted to FINRA regarding information in IAPD;
- any applicable qualification examinations passed by investment adviser representatives; and
- certain designations (*e.g.*, Certified Financial Planner, Certified Financial Analyst) reported to FINRA by the applicable designating authority.

Investment advisers register with the Commission by filing the two-part Form ADV, and withdraw from registration by filing a Form ADV-W. Regulators use Part 1 of Form ADV to process registrations and manage regulatory and examination programs.[85] Part 2A of Form ADV, known as the "brochure," is intended for advisory clients and also provides information used by the Commission's examination program.[86] Part 2B requires investment advisers to provide clients and prospective clients with a "brochure supplement" describing the educational background, business experience, and disciplinary history (if any) of specified individuals providing advisory services to a particular client.[87]

Investment advisers must update Part 1 of their Form ADV at least annually, within ninety days of their fiscal year end, or more often as needed to report certain disciplinary actions or specified changes to the adviser's services or contact information.[88] Part 1 of Form ADV uses a check-the-box, multiple-choice, question-and-answer format to describe the adviser's business. It provides details on persons who own and control the advisory firm, including whether the firm or any of its current personnel has been disciplined in the past ten years in any criminal, civil, or regulatory actions, or in foreign or military courts.[89] In 2000, the Commission substantially amended Part 1 of the form to accommodate electronic filing,[90] and divided it into two sections, with the first to be completed by all investment advisers and the second by state registered advisers.[91]

For advisory firms, the IAPD report generally displays the firm's completed Form ADV. Nearly all of the information collected on Form ADV with respect to investment advisers is made publicly available through IAPD.[92] The first item on Form ADV includes certain identifying information, including, for example: the full legal name of the firm; its registration number; its address; the days and times of normal business operations; whether it has a Web address; and whether it is registered with any foreign regulatory authority. The second item on the form covers the firm's U.S. registrations and notice filings. Item 3 on the form covers how the firm is organized and when its fiscal year ends. Item 4 covers whether the firm is a successor to a previously registered investment adviser. Item 5 contains information about the adviser's business, such as the number of employees and clients, the types of clients, the amount of assets the firm manages, and compensation agreements.

Item 6 covers other business activities of the adviser, including broker-dealer operations. Item 7 covers financial industry affiliations, such as with another investment adviser or broker-dealer. Item 8 covers the firm's participation or interest in client transactions. Item 9 covers how the firm handles custody of customers' cash or securities. Item 10 identifies who controls the adviser. Item 11 covers the adviser's regulatory and disciplinary history. Item 12 applies if the firm qualifies as a small business. Investors may click through each item to get to the next item of the form or may navigate to specific items of the form through a menu located on each page; there is no summary of the information.

Part 2A of Form ADV (the "brochure") requires some of the same information contained in Part 1, in a narrative format, as well as information on business practices, fees, and conflicts of interest that the investment adviser may have with clients. As discussed, the Commission requires investment advisers to deliver the brochure directly to clients and prospective clients before or at the time of entering into an investment advisory contract, and each year thereafter to provide clients with either a copy of the current (updated) brochure, or a summary of material changes to the brochure that includes an offer to provide a copy of the current brochure.[93] Because material changes are required to be communicated to investors, they need not access IAPD solely to apprise themselves of such developments.

Under 2010 amendments to Form ADV and related rules, most SEC-registered advisers are required to have a Part 2A brochure filed electronically by April 1, 2011.[94] The brochures, which will use a standardized format to "facilitate investors' comparison of multiple advisers," will be available in IAPD as PDF documents.[95] Brochures already are posted on IAPD for advisers that file them electronically on a voluntary basis.

The 2010 amendments also required changes to the content of brochures themselves, specifying eighteen items that must be presented in a plain English, narrative format.[96] They are:

- Item 1. Cover Page
- Item 2. Material Changes
- Item 3. Table of Contents
- Item 4. Advisory Business
- Item 5. Fees and Compensation
- Item 6. Performance-Based Fees and Side-by-Side Management
- Item 7. Types of Clients
- Item 8. Methods of Analysis, Investment Strategies and Risk of Loss
- Item 9. Disciplinary Information
- Item 10. Other Financial Industry Activities and Affiliations
- Item 11. Code of Ethics, Participation or Interest in Client Transactions and Personal Trading
- Item 12. Brokerage Practices
- Item 13. Review of Accounts
- Item 14. Client Referrals and Other Compensation
- Item 15. Custody
- Item 16. Investment Discretion
- Item 17. Voting Client Securities
- Item 18. Financial Information

The Commission's 2010 rule amendments require investment advisers to provide clients with a Part 2B brochure supplement detailing the educational background, business experience, and disciplinary history (if any) of specified individuals providing advisory services to a particular client.[97] Investment advisers registered with the Commission are not required to file Part 2B brochure supplements electronically through IARD, and the brochure supplements are not available on IAPD unless voluntarily filed through IARD.

## C. IAPD Format and Usage

Just as BrokerCheck allows users to search for a broker-dealer or a registered representative, IAPD permits users to search for an advisory firm or an investment adviser representative by name or registration number. Advisory firm searches display complete registration data on Part 1 of the firm's Form ADV and the brochure or brochures the adviser has filed. In contrast, IAPD reports on investment adviser representatives use the same format as BrokerCheck, providing a summary and a more detailed report. A link to BrokerCheck is provided on the IAPD Web site for dually registered investment adviser representatives, whose records are contained in both databases.

The summary page on IAPD for investment adviser representatives contains the same categories of information that appear on BrokerCheck for registered representatives – current employer, qualifications, registration and employment history, and disclosure events – presented in a slightly different format. The IAPD summary shows if the investment adviser representative also is registered as a registered representative, and links to BrokerCheck.

In the second quarter of 2010, there were approximately 188,572 visits to IAPD. For 2009, visits totaled approximately 1.31 million. This was an increase from approximately 1.16 million in 2008.[98] The Commission is unable to identify the number of unique visitors to IAPD, or the type of visitor, because IAPD does not place "cookies" on the computers of those using IAPD.[99]

# VI. Comparative Nature of Information Disclosed in BrokerCheck and IAPD

There are conceptual and operational differences in the way that information is made publicly available to investors regarding broker-dealers and investment advisers and their associated persons, depending on whether data about the broker-dealer, registered representative, investment adviser, or investment adviser representative are contained in BrokerCheck, in IAPD, or both.[100] For example, BrokerCheck information generally is derived from data obtained through Forms – BD, BDW, U4, U5, U6, and BR – that broker-dealers, registered representatives, and regulators complete as part of the securities industry registration and licensing process and currently file through CRD. This generally includes information about current and former members, current registered representatives, and persons who were associated with a member in the preceding ten years, and information about persons who were formerly associated with a member, but who have not been associated with a member within the preceding ten years, but who nevertheless meet certain criteria.[101] FINRA is not required to make publicly available through BrokerCheck all CRD information submitted by broker-dealers and registered representatives.

IAPD essentially reproduces all of the information contained in the Form ADV and filed through IARD. This broad disclosure regime includes, among other things, narrative brochures that address the adviser's business and conflicts of interest, details about the persons who own and control the advisory firm, including whether the firm or any of its current personnel has been disciplined in the past ten years in any criminal, civil, or regulatory actions, or in foreign or military courts as well as pending disciplinary events.[102] Investment advisers are required to deliver the brochure and any brochure supplements directly to their clients and prospective clients before or at the time of entering into an investment advisory contract, and annually thereafter to provide clients with either a copy of the current (updated) brochure, or a summary of material changes to the brochure that includes an offer to provide a copy of the current brochure.[103] Moreover, because material changes to the brochure are required to be communicated to existing and prospective advisory clients, those persons need not access IAPD to learn of such changes. The Staff has attempted to take into account the nature of these two disclosure regimes in formulating its recommendations.

# VII. RECOMMENDATIONS

The Staff makes the following recommendations. In the near-term, *i.e.*, in the eighteen-month implementation period, the Staff recommends: (1) unifying BrokerCheck and IAPD search results; (2) adding a ZIP code search or other indicator of location function to BrokerCheck and IAPD; and (3) adding educational content to BrokerCheck and IAPD. The Staff also recommends that, subsequent to the eighteen-month implementation period, Commission staff and FINRA continue to analyze, including through investor testing, the feasibility and advisability of expanding BrokerCheck to include information currently available in CRD, as well as the method and format of publishing that information; and that Commission staff continue to evaluate expanding IAPD content and the method and format of publishing that content, including through investor testing.

## A. Near-Term Recommendations

The near-term recommendations, as described in greater detail below, involve unifying BrokerCheck and IAPD search results, adding a ZIP code search or other indicator of location function to BrokerCheck and IAPD, and adding educational content to BrokerCheck and IAPD.

### *1. Further Centralizing Access to CRD and IARD Through Use of a Unified Search Function*

As noted earlier, the primary advantage of centralized access to registration information is that all of the data in the two systems would be in one place, making it easier for investors to obtain useful data. As described above, the current disclosure system comprises two distinct registration databases, requiring investors to know which database to search: BrokerCheck or IAPD.[104] For investors who do not know whether their financial services provider is registered as a broker-dealer or an investment adviser, knowing where to conduct a background search may be problematic.[105] Moreover, not all financial services providers are required to register, including some service providers in the mortgage brokerage, banking, futures trading, or insurance industries. Some are exempt from registration or operate outside the Commission's oversight. Centralizing access would make it more likely that investors could find data about a financial services provider who at any time was registered as a registered representative or investment adviser representative, whether or not they knew the provider's registration status.

For the reasons above, a single system for searching for data on broker-dealers, investment advisers, and their associated persons may yield benefits in the long-term. However, given the time constraints imposed by the Dodd-Frank Act, maintaining the current separate databases, but unifying the search results, seems more feasible in the near-term. This approach would maintain the current CRD and IARD databases and the current BrokerCheck and IAPD Web sites, but each system would be modified to search the other's database and to return results from both.[106]

There are several benefits to investors from unifying search results from the BrokerCheck and IAPD systems. It would eliminate the possibility that an investor would search for records about a broker-dealer or investment adviser, but fail to locate them because the investor chose the wrong database to search. It would also make the search process more efficient by eliminating the need to search two separate databases. Further, there would be no need to develop or promote a new Web site, making this approach less costly than the second option described below. Finally, the current level of usability would be maintained.

The Staff also considered two other approaches: (i) collapsing the two systems into a single public database; and (ii) creating an additional third Web site that would serve as a search portal for the systems. In the near-term, given the eighteen-month implementation period and other considerations discussed below, the Staff instead recommends maintaining the current separate databases but unifying the search results.

***Collapsing the two systems.*** For the reasons above, a single system for searching for data about financial services providers may have long-term benefits. Creating a single public disclosure database by merging BrokerCheck and IAPD would facilitate investor access to data regarding financial services providers registered with the Commission. The advantage of this approach, as with our recommendation of a unified search function, is that it could make it easier for investors to access information because all of the information would be housed in a single database with a single point of access.

However, this approach presents significant issues that could be difficult to resolve expeditiously. Those issues include determining the potential costs and benefits of merging the two databases, the impact of such a merger on database ownership and the need for agreement among FINRA, NASAA, and the Commission, and the effect of a merger on the usability of a combined system. In addition, this option could entail potentially significant costs to re-engineer and redesign the sites and to market the new database.

***Creating a third Web site portal.*** Another approach would be to maintain BrokerCheck and IAPD in their current forms, but create a new Web site that would provide a single public disclosure gateway to them. This portal would not require users to know whether they should use BrokerCheck or IAPD. The creation of a third, separate route to the existing databases might pose fewer issues than an outright merging of BrokerCheck and IAPD because each system would remain independent. However, developing a new Web site would take additional resources, further time to acclimate investors to the new Web site as a source of information (particularly given the widespread use of BrokerCheck), and there would be questions to resolve, such as who would own and maintain the new Web site.

### *2. Add Search by ZIP Code or Other Indicator of Location*

BrokerCheck and IAPD are designed to search for an individual or firm by name or registration number, which is useful only to investors who already have a broker-dealer or investment adviser, or who wish to research a particular person or firm, for example, one that has "cold-called" or otherwise solicited, or been referred to, them.[107] The systems are not, however, as useful for more general research about financial services providers. For example, they do not easily permit investors to locate and compare nearby financial services providers because they lack a function that would allow investors to search for a broker-dealer or investment adviser by ZIP code or other indicator of location. A search by ZIP code function might be helpful to investors who are seeking to hire a financial services provider by identifying those financial services providers who are located close enough to visit in person, or to compare an individual they have hired already with others nearby providing similar services. The Internet is now commonly used as a research tool, with approximately 58% of adults conducting research online about the products and services they buy,[108] a level that rises to approximately 88% for those with a household income of $75,000 or more.[109] However, the Internet is not commonly used to assist in the search for a financial services provider.[110]

Adding a search by ZIP code function to BrokerCheck and IAPD may raise concerns, however. One concern is that providing the names of financial firms or financial services providers on a regulatory site would be viewed by investors as an endorsement of the individuals or firms identified by the search. To help address this concern, a prominent disclaimer could be added to inform users that search results do not constitute an endorsement. A second concern is that a ZIP code search function could encourage third parties to extract data from BrokerCheck and IAPD for repackaging and sale. While the Staff does not necessarily oppose the widespread dissemination of registration information, some methods that third parties use to extract data, such as data-scraping,[111] can interfere with the efficient performance of the systems. Although data-scraping and other technology issues related to a search by ZIP code function pose challenges, these obstacles do not appear to be insurmountable because technologies and protocols currently exist that are widely used by commercial firms to prevent the unauthorized acquisition of information, proprietary or otherwise. Implementing a search by ZIP code function for BrokerCheck would require FINRA to make programming changes to BrokerCheck; adding this function to IAPD would require programming changes with Commission authorization.

### *3. Add Educational Content*

The Staff recommends that the BrokerCheck and IAPD Web sites be modified to add online educational materials, including links and definitions of terms that may be unfamiliar to individual investors. The definitions could be displayed through a rollover, hyperlinks, or other technology. Currently, BrokerCheck and IAPD both contain glossaries with definitions of terms used on the sites. For example, the BrokerCheck glossary includes terms that frequently appear on BrokerCheck reports, such as “arbitration,” “branch office,” “clearing firm,” “judgment,” and “lien.” The defined terms also cover forms, including Form BD, Form BDW, Form U4, Form U5 and Form U6, providing explanations of each. The BrokerCheck glossary explains some, but not all, industry examinations, including supervisory examinations. Similarly, the glossary on IAPD covers terms commonly used in the advisory industry, such as “client,” “discretionary authority,” “performance-based fee,” and “wrap fee program.” The defined terms also cover terms used on the forms, such as “advisory affiliate,” “investment-related,” and “management persons.” Terms used by regulators, such as “notice filing,” and legal terms appear in the glossary as well.

The Staff recommends that both Web sites include additional glossary definitions and explanatory material, written in a succinct and accessible manner. Investor testing or other means of soliciting investor input could help determine the terms that investors find confusing and would like to have explained and defined.

## B. Intermediate-Term Recommendation – Continued Analysis of BrokerCheck and IAPD

The Staff also recommends that, subsequent to the eighteen-month implementation period, Commission staff and FINRA continue to analyze, including through investor testing, the feasibility and advisability of expanding

BrokerCheck to include information currently available in CRD, as well as the method and format of publishing that information; and that Commission staff continue to evaluate expanding IAPD content and the method and format of publishing that content, including through investor testing.

Access to information filed on CRD and IARD can help investors make better decisions about their selection or evaluation of broker-dealers and investment advisers, and the Staff believes that such information should be disclosed to the public. The Commission has long expressed the view that registration information about financial services providers is key to making sound investment decisions.[112] As described above, IAPD and BrokerCheck are systems that provide investors important data about the financial services providers on whom they will rely in helping to meet their investment goals. While the Commission has stated that BrokerCheck is "a valuable tool for an investor to use to get information about a firm or a registered person with whom the investor is considering doing business," the Commission nonetheless has "urge[d] investors to check with each state where the firm has done business or where the sales person has been registered to obtain a complete picture of his or her disciplinary history."[113] Moreover, the Commission previously has encouraged FINRA to consider increasing the amount of information available on BrokerCheck.[114]

As discussed, regulators currently collect more information on registration forms than is made publicly available on BrokerCheck. For example, BrokerCheck excludes information reported on Form U5 concerning the reason for a registered representative's termination and any comments from the former registered representative regarding that termination reported on Form U5. Also, as discussed, FINRA excludes from BrokerCheck, generally, information on Form U4 for registered representatives who have terminated registration more than ten years ago.[115] Historical filings are another type of content that may be of interest to investors. BrokerCheck and IAPD provide only the most recent filings by broker-dealers, investment advisers, and their associated persons; they do not provide access to previous filings. Expanding BrokerCheck and IAPD to include registration data from previously filed registration forms, or amendments to them, would permit investors to review a firm's filing history and the changes the firm has undergone over time. Investor input could help determine whether investors would find any of this additional information useful.[116]

Similarly, investor input could help determine whether to revise formatting on the BrokerCheck or IAPD Web sites. For example, focus group testing may be an effective way to evaluate the usefulness of summary disclosure compared to full presentation of original documents, such as Form ADV. Such testing could also help determine whether investors would prefer to have the option to view a summary page on IAPD for advisory firms, similar to the summary data available on BrokerCheck and for investment adviser representatives on IAPD. Another possible modification to the BrokerCheck and IAPD Web sites is to hyperlink CRD numbers and SEC file numbers to information relating to owners, officers and affiliates associated with those numbers. The addition of these hyperlinks could make other business activities of broker-dealer and investment advisers, and their owners and officers, more transparent to investors. In addition, providing hyperlinks to content now available in BrokerCheck, which investors may obtain by clicking on the separate filings, could also provide investors with helpful information.

## CONCLUSION

Individual investors need useful tools to help them make important decisions about hiring and retaining broker-dealers and investment advisers. While BrokerCheck and IAPD currently are very helpful to investors, the recommendations in this study are intended to make these systems more accessible and useful to investors. This study responds to the requirement of Section 919B of the Act, which mandates that the Commission analyze the advantages and disadvantages of further centralizing access to registration information contained in CRD and IARD, identify data pertinent to investors and the method and format for displaying and publishing the data to enhance their accessibility by, and utility to, investors. It also responds to the requirement to provide recommendations to improve investor access to registration information and to identify additional information that could be made publicly available.

## End Notes

[1] Pub. L. No. 111-203, 124 Stat. 1376 (2010).

[2] Section 202(a)(17) of the Investment Advisers Act of 1940 [15 U.S.C. 80b-2(a)(17)] defines "person associated with an investment adviser" in relevant part as "any partner, officer, or director of such investment adviser (or any person performing similar functions), or any person directly or indirectly controlling or controlled by such investment adviser, including any employee of such investment adviser . . . ."

[3] Section 3(a)(18) of the Securities Exchange Act of 1934 [15 U.S.C. 78c(a)(18)] defines "person associated with a broker or dealer" in relevant part as "any partner, officer, director, or

branch manager of such broker or dealer (or any person occupying a similar status or performing similar functions), any person directly or indirectly controlling, controlled by, or under common control with such broker or dealer, or any employee of such broker or dealer . . . ."

[4] The Staff reviewed, among other things, prior Commission releases, comment letters pertaining to other relevant Commission regulatory actions, and empirical data obtained from FINRA and NASAA. The Commission has provided the opportunity for the public to comment generally on regulatory initiatives to be undertaken in response to the Dodd-Frank Act. *See* request for public comments on SEC regulatory initiatives under the Dodd-Frank Act at http://www.sec.gov/spotlight/regreformcomments.shtml. There were no public comments submitted regarding the Section 919B study. While the Staff did not speak directly with individual investors in connection with this study, the Staff recommends (as described in greater detail in Section VII) investor testing or other means of soliciting investor input related to registration information as part of the Commission study of the financial literacy of investors required by Section 917 of the Dodd-Frank Act.

[5] NASAA is a voluntary association whose membership consists of sixty-seven state, provincial, and territorial securities administrators in the fifty U.S. states, the District of Columbia, Puerto Rico, the U.S. Virgin Islands, Canada, and Mexico.

[6] The Chairman of the Commission did not participate.

[7] BrokerCheck is the online application, developed by FINRA, through which the public may obtain information regarding current and former FINRA member firms, and current and former associated persons of FINRA member firms. The Central Registration Depository (CRD®) is the securities industry online registration and licensing database developed by FINRA in consultation with the states. Information in CRD is obtained through forms that broker-dealers, registered representatives, and regulators complete as part of the securities industry registration and licensing process. The information made available through BrokerCheck is derived from CRD.

[8] The IARD database is comprised of information concerning all SEC-registered investment advisers, as well as most advisers that have registered or applied for registration with state regulators since 2001. IAPD provides online access to records for SEC and state-registered advisers, and was expanded in mid-2010 to include records for registered investment adviser representatives.

[9] *See, e.g.*, Investment Advisers Act Release No. 3060 (July 28, 2010) [75 FR 49234 n.5 (Aug. 12, 2010)] (adopting amendments to Form ADV) (stating that "the disclosure clients and prospective clients receive is critical to their ability to make an informed decision about whether to engage an adviser and, having engaged the adviser, to manage the relationship"); Investment Advisers Act Release No. 1897 (Sept. 12, 2000) [65 FR 57438, 57445 (Sept. 22, 2000)](adopting rules and rule amendments requiring electronic filing by investment advisers) (stating that the amendments were "necessary" to, among other things, "develop a database of information about advisers that is easily accessible to investors").

[10] *See* Investment Advisers Act Release No. 3129 (Dec. 28, 2010) [76 FR 255, 256 (Jan. 4, 2011)] (extending compliance dates for delivery of certain brochure supplements). Generally, all investment advisers registered with the Commission as of December 31, 2010, and having a fiscal year ending on December 31, 2010 through April 30, 2011, have until July 31, 2011 to begin delivering brochure supplements to new and prospective clients, and until September 30, 2011 to deliver brochure supplements to existing clients. *Id.* Brochure supplement delivery deadlines remain unchanged for existing registered investment advisers with fiscal years ending after April 30, 2011. *Id.* Newly-registered investment advisers filing their applications for registration from January 1, 2011 through April 30, 2011 generally have until May 1, 2011 to begin delivering brochure supplements to new and prospective clients, and until July 1, 2011 to deliver brochure supplements to existing clients. *Id.* Brochure supplement delivery deadlines for investment advisers filing registration applications with the Commission after April 30, 2011 remain unchanged. *Id.*

[11] Exchange Act Release No. 59916 (May 13, 2009) [74 FR 23750, 23754 (May 20, 2009)] (approving rule change relating to changes to Forms U4, U5, and FINRA Rule 8312 (SR-FINRA-2009-008)).

[12] *See, e.g.*, Exchange Act Release No. 61002 (Nov. 13, 2009) [74 FR 61193 (Nov. 23, 2009)] (approving rule change relating to BrokerCheck disclosure (SR-FINRA-2009-050)); Exchange Act Release No. 55127(January 18, 2007) [72 FR 03455 (January 25, 2007)] (approving SR-NASD-2003-168).

[13] *See* http://www.sec.gov/investor/pubs/askquestions.htm. A recent national study of the financial capability of American adults sponsored by the FINRA Investor Education Foundation found that only 15% of respondents who have used a financial services provider in the last five years claimed to have checked the background, registration, or license of a financial services provider. *See Financial Capability in the United States*, at 46 (FINRA Investor Education Foundation, Dec. 1, 2009). As this statistic indicates, continued education is warranted to help investors better understand the importance of conducting a thorough review of available information on financial services providers by using BrokerCheck and/or IAPD.

[14] *See* http://www.sec.gov/investor/pubs/inws.htm

[15] *See* http://www.sec.gov/investor/pubs/askquestions.htm

[16] *See* http://www.sec.gov/investor/brokers.htm

[17] *See* Exchange Act Release No. 62476 (July 8, 2010) [75 FR 41254 (July 15, 2010)] (approving amendments to FINRA's BrokerCheck disclosure rule (SR-FINRA-2010-012)).

[18] Investment Advisers Act Release No. 3110 n.123 (Nov. 19, 2010) [75 FR 77052, 77062 n.123 (Dec. 10, 2010)] (proposing rules implementing amendments to the Advisers Act).

[19] Investment Advisers Act Release No. 3060 (July 28, 2010) [75 FR 49234, 49234 (Aug. 12, 2010)] (adopting rule amendments to Form ADV).

[20] *See* Study on Investment Advisers and Broker-Dealers, as required by Section 913 of the Dodd-Frank Act ("Section 913 Study") at 137, available at http://www.sec.gov/news/studies/2011/913studyfinal.pdf (discussing the disclosure requirements of Form ADV and Form BD).

[21] *See* the National Securities Market Improvement Act of 1996, Pub. L. No. 104-290, 110 Stat. 3438 (1996).

[22] *See* Advisers Act Section 203A(a)(1)(A) [15 U.S.C. 80b-3a(a)(1)(A)].

[23] *See* Investment Advisers Act Release No. 3110 (Nov. 19, 2010) [75 FR 77052 (Dec. 10, 2010)] (proposing rules implementing amendments to the Advisers Act).

[24] *See* Letter from FINRA (Nov. 3, 2010) (File No. 4-606) (regarding obligations of brokers, dealers, and investment advisers).

[25] Based on data obtained from IARD on Nov. 8, 2010.

[26] *Id.*

[27] Based on data obtained from FINRA on Nov. 3, 2010.

[28] Note, however, that Wyoming does not have a statutory requirement for investment adviser registration.

[29] For example, Oregon provides online access to information on investment advisers registered in the state. *See* the Oregon Division of Finance and Corporate Securities Web site at http://www4.cbs.state.or.us/ex/dfcs/dfcslic/adviser/.

[30] *See* Exchange Act Sections (3)(a)(4)(A) and (3)(a)(5)(A) [15 U.S.C. 78c(a)(4)(A) and 78c (a)(5)(A)].

[31] On July 26, 2007, the Commission approved a proposed rule change by NASD to amend its Certificate of Incorporation to reflect its name change to FINRA, in connection with the consolidation of its member firm regulatory functions with NYSE Regulation, Inc. *See* Exchange Act Rel. No. 56145 (Jul. 26, 2007) [72 FR 42190 (Aug. 1, 2007)]. For purposes of this study, the acronym "FINRA" will be used throughout except to refer to NASD rules and notices that FINRA continues to use.

[32] *See* NASAA's Web site at http://www.nasaa.org/industry. NASAA also includes hyperlinks to BrokerCheck and IAPD on its investor education Web page. *See* NASAA's investor education Web page at http://www.nasaa.org/ investor_education/11080.cfm .

[33] *See id.*

[34] Information on the Uniform Forms is available at http://www.finra.org/industry .

[35] *See* Exchange Act Release No. 25604 (April 20, 1988) [53 FR 14878 (April 26, 1988)] (Notice of Filing and Immediate Effectiveness of File No. SR-NASD-88-14).

[36] *See* Exchange Act Release No. 61927 (Apr. 16, 2010) [75 FR 21064 (Apr. 22, 2010)] (proposing amendments to FINRA's BrokerCheck disclosure rule (SR-FINRA-2010-012)).

[37] *See* FINRA's Web site at www.finra.org/Industry/Compliance/Registration/CRD/index.htm.

[38] *See* NASD Notice to Members 02-74 (Nov. 2002) (requesting comment on Public Information Review Initiative).

[39] *See* Exchange Act Release No. 60462 (August 7, 2009) [74 FR 41470 (August 17, 2009)] (FINRA's proposed rule change to its BrokerCheck disclosure rule (SR-FINRA-2009-050)).

[40] *See* Military Personnel Financial Service Protection Act, Pub. L. No. 109-290, 120 Stat. 1317 (2006).

[41] In October 2010, the BrokerCheck database covered approximately 637,347 registered representatives and approximately 4,698 registered broker-dealer firms (based on data obtained from FINRA on Oct. 8, 2010). Of the firms, approximately 842, or approximately 18.4%, also were registered as investment advisers with the Commission or a state (based on data obtained from FINRA on Nov. 3, 2010). There were approximately 12,440 formerly-registered broker-dealers in the database in October 2010 (based on data obtained from FINRA on Oct. 8, 2010). In October 2010, BrokerCheck displayed records for approximately 182,582 former registered representatives, with approximately 32,000 of the records, or approximately 17.5%, permanently available (based on data obtained from FINRA on Oct. 8, 2010). In 2009, more than 20 million searches were conducted through BrokerCheck.

[42] A registered representative is subject to a final regulatory action if, among other things, he or she was: convicted of or pled guilty or no contest to certain crimes; subject to a civil injunction involving investment-related activity; found in a civil court to have been involved in a violation of investment-related statues or regulations, or named as a respondent or defendant in an investment-related, consumer initiated arbitration or civil lawsuit that alleged he or she committed a sales practice violation and resulted in an award or civil judgment against him or her. *See* Exchange Act Release No. 62476 (July 8, 2010) [75 FR 41254 (July 15, 2010)] (approving amendments to FINRA's BrokerCheck disclosure rule (SR-FINRA-2010-012)).

[43] Broker-dealers must update CRD no later than thirty days after they learn that an update is required and in some instances, within ten days. *See* NYSE Rule 351(b) and NASD Rule 3070(b).

[44] *See* Exchange Act Release No. 42402 (Feb. 7, 2000) [65 FR 7582 (Feb. 15, 2000)] (approving amendments to NASD's Public Disclosure Program (SR-NASD-99-45)).

[45] *See* Exchange Act Release No. 55127 (Jan. 18, 2007) [72 FR 3455 (Jan. 25, 2007)] (approving rule change relating to BrokerCheck disclosure (SR-NASD-2003-168)).

[46] Historic complaints are customer complaints that were reported on a uniform registration form that are more than two years old and that have not been settled or adjudicated and customer complaints, arbitrations, or litigations that have been settled for an amount less than the specified dollar amount (identified on the customer complaint question) and are therefore no longer reportable on a uniform registration form. *See* Exchange Act Release No. 62476 (July 8, 2010) [75 FR 41254 (July 15, 2010)] (approving amendments relating to BrokerCheck disclosure (SR-FINRA-2010-012)).

[47] *See* Exchange Act Release No. 61002 (Nov. 13, 2009) [74 FR 61193 (Nov. 23, 2009)] (approving rule change relating to BrokerCheck disclosure (SR-FINRA-2009-050)).

[48] In approving the FINRA rule filing, the Commission stated that it "will help members of the public to protect themselves from unscrupulous people." *See* Exchange Act Release No. 62476 (July 8, 2010) [75 FR 41254, 41257 (July 15, 2010)] (approving amendments relating to BrokerCheck disclosure (SR-FINRA-2010-012)). In approving the proposed rule change, the Commission stated that "such information is relevant to investors and members of the public who wish to educate themselves with respect to the professional history of a formerly associated person. Formerly associated persons, although no longer in the securities industry in a registered capacity, may work in other investment-related industries, such as financial planning," or "may seek to attain other positions of trust with potential investors. Disclosure of such person's record, while he was in the securities industry via BrokerCheck should help members of the public decide whether to rely on his advice or expertise or do business with him." *Id.*

[49] *See* Exchange Act Release No. 61002 (Nov. 13, 2009) [74 FR 61193 (Nov. 23, 2009)] (approving rule change relating to BrokerCheck disclosure (SR-FINRA-2009-050)).

[50] *See supra* note 48.

[51] Exchange Act Release No. 62476 (July 8, 2010) [75 FR 41254 (July 15, 2010)].

[52] Exchange Act Release No. 62476 (July 8, 2010) [75 FR 41254 (July 15, 2010)].

[53] *See* FINRA Rule 8312(d).

[54] *See* FINRA Rule 8312(b).

[55] *See* FINRA Rule 8312(d).

[56] *See* FINRA Rule 8312(c).

[57] *See* FINRA Rule 8312(b)(1).

[58] FINRA has stated that it excludes such information because the passing grade varies from examination to examination and can change over time, and that examination scores are not designed to predict an individual's job performance or compliance record. *Id.*

[59] Based on data obtained from FINRA on Nov. 3, 2010.

[60] Based on data obtained from FINRA on Oct. 8, 2010.

[61] Although the BrokerCheck Web site includes a link to a voluntary survey that visitors may access to provide demographic data to FINRA for its internal use, it is unclear whether, and how many, visitors to the BrokerCheck Web site actually access and respond to the survey.

[62] *See* Advisers Act Section 202(a)(11) [15 U.S.C. 80b-2(a)(11)].

[63] *See* Investment Advisers Act Release No. 3060 (July 28, 2010) [75 FR 49234 n.5 (Aug. 12, 2010)] (adopting rule amendments to Form ADV).

[64] *See* Investment Advisers Act Release No. 73 (June 25, 1954).

[65] *See* Investment Advisers Act Release No. 991 (Oct. 15, 1985) [50 FR 42903 (Oct. 23, 1985)]. The uniform Form ADV became effective on January 1, 1986.

[66] *Id.*

[67] *See* Investment Advisers Act Release No. 664 (Jan. 30, 1979) [44 FR 7370 (Feb. 7, 1979)]. *See also* Rule 204-3(a) under the Advisers Act [17 CFR 275.204-3(a)].

[68] *See* Rule 204-3 under the Advisers Act [17 CFR 275.204-3].

[69] *See* Investment Advisers Act Release No. 3060 (July 28, 2010) [75 FR 49234 n.5 (Aug. 12, 2010)] (adopting rule amendments to Form ADV).

[70] As discussed in greater detail in Section V.B below, the brochure supplement describes the educational background, business experience, and disciplinary history (if any) of specified individuals providing advisory services to a particular client.

[71] Pub. L. No. 104-290, 110 Stat. 3438 (1996). NSMIA is codified in relevant part as Section 203A of the Advisers Act [15 U.S.C. 80b-3a].

[72] The Commission and the states retained general antifraud enforcement authority over the advisers that were not registered with them.

[73] Advisers Act Section 203A(a)(1)(A) [15 U.S.C. 80b-3a(a)(1)(A)].

[74] *See* Section 410 of the Dodd-Frank Act; Advisers Act Section 203A [15 U.S.C. 80b-3]; Investment Advisers Act Release No. 3110 (Nov. 19, 2010) [75 FR 77052 (Dec. 10, 2010)] (proposing rules implementing amendments to the Advisers Act to effectuate certain

provisions of the Dodd-Frank Act, including requiring, among other things, hedge funds and other private funds to register with the Commission).

[75] Pub. L. No. 104-290, 110 Stat. 3438 (1996). *See also* Investment Advisers Act Release No. 1897 (Sept. 12, 2000) [65 FR 57438 (Sept. 22, 2000)] (adopting rules and rule amendments requiring electronic filing by investment advisers).

[76] Investment Advisers Act Release No. 1897 (Sept. 12, 2000) [65 FR 57438, 57445 (Sept. 22, 2000)](adopting rules and rule amendments requiring electronic filing by investment advisers) (stating that the amendments were "necessary" to, among other things, "develop a database of information about advisers that is easily accessible to investors").

[77] *See* IARD Web site at http://www.iard.com/WhatIsIARD.asp.

[78] *See* Investment Advisers Act Release No. 3060 (July 28, 2010) [75 FR 49234 (Aug. 12, 2010)] (adopting rule amendments to Form ADV).

[79] *See* Investment Advisers Act Release No. 3110 (Nov. 19, 2010) [75 FR 77052 (Dec. 10, 2010)] (proposing rules implementing amendments to the Advisers Act to effectuate certain provisions of the Dodd-Frank Act, including requiring, among other things, managers of hedge funds and other private funds to register with the Commission).

[80] *See* Investment Advisers Act Release No. 3060 (July 28, 2010) [75 FR 49234 (Aug. 12, 2010)] (adopting amendments to Form ADV).

[81] *Id.*

[82] Based on data obtained from IARD on Nov. 8, 2010. SEC registration data are as of Nov. 1, 2010. State registration data are as of July 1, 2010.

[83] *See* Investment Advisers Act Release No. 3060 (July 28, 2010) [75 FR 49234 (Aug. 12, 2010)] (adopting amendments to Form ADV).

[84] Form ADV-E is the form that is required to be completed by investment advisers that have custody of client funds or securities and that are subject to an annual surprise examination.

[85] *See* Investment Advisers Act Release No. 3060 (July 28, 2010) [75 FR 49234 (Aug. 12, 2010)] (adopting amendments to Form ADV).

[86] *Id.*

[87] *Id.*

[88] *Id.*

[89] Investment Advisers Act Release No. 1897 (Sept. 12, 2000) [65 FR 57438, 57445 (Sept. 22, 2000)].

[90] *Id.*

[91] *Id.*

[92] Two categories of information filed with IARD but excluded from IAPD are historical filings and withdrawal forms. An investment adviser's registration status, however, does reflect withdrawal form filings. In addition, certain personally identifiable information such as Social Security numbers and private residence addresses of investment adviser representatives are not available on IAPD.

[93] *See* Rule 204-3 under the Advisers Act [17 CFR 275.204-3].

[94] *See* Investment Advisers Act Release No. 3060 (July 28, 2010) [75 FR 49234 (Aug. 12, 2010)] (adopting amendments to Form ADV).

[95] *Id.*

[96] *Id.*

[97] *Id.*

[98] Based on data obtained from FINRA on July 28, 2010.

[99] *See* IARD Web site at http://www.iard.com .

[100] The Staff recognizes that additional investor education and promotion of BrokerCheck and IAPD may be required to encourage investors to use those two systems. Further investigation into investor usage of BrokerCheck and IAPD is anticipated in connection with the Commission's study pursuant to Section 917 of the Dodd-Frank Act, regarding financial literacy among investors. *See also* Section 913 Study.

[101] *See supra* Section IV.B.

[102] Note that BrokerCheck and IAPD "may disclose slightly different information regarding [h]istoric [c]omplaints of those financial services professionals that are dually registered as brokers and investment advisers." Exchange Act Release No. 61927 n.20 (Apr. 16, 2010) [75 FR 21064 (Apr. 22, 2010)] (proposing amendments to FINRA's BrokerCheck disclosure rule and discussing IAPD-I, the database that provides public registration and licensing information about natural persons who are registered as investment advisers with the states (SR-FINRA-2010-012)). For dually registered firms and representatives, the BrokerCheck report shows that information about the firm or the individual is available through IAPD, and the IAPD report shows that information about the firm or individual is available through BrokerCheck. In either case, the report includes a link to the other database. Historic customer complaints for investment adviser representatives that are made publicly available on IAPD date back to March 18, 2002, which is the date that IARD began accepting filings for investment adviser representative registration. *See* Exchange Act Release No. 61927 n.20 (Apr. 16, 2010) [75 FR 21064 (Apr. 22, 2010)]. BrokerCheck makes publicly available historic complaints, including those archived after the implementation of Web CRD on August 16, 1999.

[103] *See* Rule 204-3 under the Advisers Act [17 CFR 275.204-3].

[104] This has led some to call for "a unified database that could track individuals," including those who are dually registered. *See* Angela A. Hung *et al.*, *Investor and Industry Perspectives on Investment Advisers and Broker-Dealers*, at 79 (RAND Institute for Civil Justice 2008) (the "RAND Report").

[105] The RAND Report found investors typically fail to distinguish between broker-dealers and investment advisers along the lines defined by federal regulations.

[106] As discussed, currently, for dually registered firms and representatives, the BrokerCheck report shows that information about the firm or the individual is available through IAPD, and the IAPD report shows that information about the firm or individual is available through BrokerCheck. In either case, the report includes a link to the other database.

[107] According to one recent survey, most people searching for a financial services firm or a financial services provider rely on referrals from family members, friends, or professionals. *See* Angela A. Hung *et al.*, *Investor Knowledge and Experience with Investment Advisers and Broker-Dealers* (RAND Institute for Civil Justice 2010). The same survey found less than 10% of those surveyed use the Internet to find a financial services firm and less than one percent use the Internet to find a financial services provider. *Id.* at 42. While family members, friends, and professionals can serve as valuable sources of information, the Staff believes that investors should evaluate thoroughly the background of any financial services provider that they use or plan to engage.

[108] *See* Jim Jansen, *Online Product Research* (Pew Internet & American Life Project at 2) (Sept. 29, 2010) (documenting the percentage of Americans who have researched a product or service online).

[109] *Id.* at 4.

[110] One way of locating information on the Internet via a search engine is to use a "local qualifier" such as a ZIP code. For example, some major financial institutions provide ZIP code search tools on their proprietary Web sites to help direct clients and prospective clients to local offices or affiliated financial services providers. Some financial trade associations also offer connections by ZIP code to certain credentialed financial services providers that they represent. Another category of financial search tools is provided by commercial Web sites that offer to link investors to the type of qualified financial services provider they are seeking based on ZIP code. These various ZIP code search tools, however, generally do not appear to provide the depth of information and detailed disclosures contained in BrokerCheck or IAPD.

[111] Data- or screen-scraping is the process of acquiring data displayed onscreen by capturing the displayed text, either manually with the "copy" command or via software. *See, e.g.*, Christopher Vidiksis, *How to Buffer Your Way Out of a Scrape: Potential Abuse of the*

*Cartoon Network v. Cablevision Decision*, 4 Brook. J. Corp. Fin. & Com. L. 139, 140 n.32 (Fall 2009) (describing variations of screen-scraping). Screen-scraping typically occurs when software developers and data aggregators employ the use of programs that rove the Internet and programmatically evaluate digitally displayed information in order to extract from it the specific information requested by a third party. *Id.* at 147. *See also* Julia Angwin and Steve Stecklow, *'Scrapers' Dig Deep for Data on Web*, Wall St. J. (Oct. 12, 2010).

[112] *See, e.g.*, Investment Advisers Act Release No. 3060 (July 28, 2010) [75 FR 49234 n.5 (Aug. 12, 2010)] (adopting amendments to Form ADV) (stating that "the disclosure clients and prospective clients receive is critical to their ability to make an informed decision about whether to engage an adviser and, having engaged the adviser, to manage the relationship.").

[113] Exchange Act Release No. 55127 (Jan. 18, 2007) [72 FR 3455, 3461 (Jan. 25, 2007)].

[114] Exchange Act Release No. 62476 (July 8, 2010) [75 FR 41254 (July 15, 2010)] (SR-FINRA-2010-012) ("The Commission urges FINRA to consider expanding the information as suggested by the commenters. This information is available from the individual states; however, it would be more accessible through BrokerCheck. The Commission urges the public to utilize all sources of information particularly, the databases of the state regulators, as well as legal search engines and records searches, in conducting a thorough search of any associated person's activities."). In addition, information about other actions that are not disclosed on BrokerCheck may be available through other public sources, such as online search engines, regulators' Web sites, and fee-based services such as Lexis or Westlaw. *Id.*

[115] *See* FINRA Rule 8312(b)(1).

[116] The Staff is unaware of any formal information-gathering regarding investors' views of BrokerCheck or IAPD.

# INDEX

## U



## V



## W



## Y